Features

- 02 — Editorial: What is City? — Roger McKinley
- 04 — Celebrate Everything You Normally Do: Will Alsop's Praxis — Will McLean
- 08 — Sensual Cities — Phil Griffin
- 12 — Palm-fringed disco: Peter Saville — Susie Stubbs
- 16 — Unknown Pleasure: The Haçienda — Jon Savage
- 40 — In the Belly of the Architect — Iain Sinclair
- 44 — Further — Iain Sinclair
- 49 — Fail Better: The art of Paul Bradley — Dan McClean
- 53 — Standing in the way of control: Superflex, tenantspin and Alan Dunn. An investigation into social media — Marie-Anne McQuay
- 57 — Singing the sound of silence — Alan Dunn
- 58 — (Sitting on a log) Imagining the SuperCity Art School — Derek Horton
- 60 — The House on the Borderland: Lesley Young, James Hutchinson and the Salford Restoration Office — Laura Mansfield

Inbetween

- 31 — Linder
- 32 — The Magnetic North

Flash Artists

- 19 — 8 key artists for Corridor8
- 20 — Isabel Nolan — Dublin
- 22 — Bob Levene — Hull
- 24 — Rachel Goodyear — Manchester / Salford
- 26 — Simon Le Ruez — Sheffield
- 28 — Freee — Sheffield / Hull / Warrington
- 30 — Matthew Houlding — Todmorden
- 36 — Rory Macbeth — Leeds
- 38 — Paul Rooney — Liverpool

Editorial

What is City?

Behind my house the intercity trains roar past, rattling the bolts of the locks in the doorframes. Goods trains that bear names such as Maersk, P&O, China Shipping and Hapag-Lloyd creak and clank past, heavy with collective weight of global commerce, squealing high pitch metallic complaints into the orange night air. The imposing bleach-white skeletal groins and trusses of a famous football stadium sits just the other side of the line, squatting at the edge of mile on mile of industrial brown field. Gradually, with the tick of an enormous and irregular clock whose hands shift in eons, the old industry is being converted into sites of cultural activity that include shopping centres, art galleries, museums, theatres and media centres. Hand in glove with this rise up the luxury flats, the dockside apartments, the affordable and unaffordable new urban terrain of signature architectural sprawl. The skyline is a symphony of cranes, penthouses and vapour trails, a tone poem of the contemporary city. This is the view that first greets the passengers on the incoming trains, the amber haze of confidence that is, for the time being, neither on stop nor go, held growling back by the shadow of a dark stain from the haemorrhaging economy.

I live in the city. I work in another. I visit yet others. I am repulsed by it, and infatuated by it, I want to escape it and I want to embrace it. I want to define it, and cannot. A part of me loves to love it, a part of me hates to hate it. I resist its embrace and embrace its resistance. I affiliate and I disassociate. I am fickle, proud and disloyal. I break my promise to the city, and it breaks my heart.

trip is filmmaker Chris Petit, who supplies the visual lodestones to Sinclair's journey.

Will Alsop is charged with inventing the term 'Super-City' to describe the region roughly arcing between Liverpool and Hull that was famously elaborated in an exhibition at the Urbis centre in 2005. Will McLean investigates his idiosyncratic architectural vision and how his radical practice developed out of his love of art, moving earth and pork pies. To accompany this writer Phil Griffin digs deeper into Alsop's practice as an artist and unearths resonating themes between the freedom he finds in this form of expression, and the parallel practice of giving form to the living environment. Is there, in the conflicting experiences of these directions, a resolution in the paring of art and architecture? Can a co-joining line be drawn that may just indicate a way to bring the future of building into harmony with the future of people and their understanding of community, ecology and commerce?

Peter Saville, in a paper to the Manchester City Council in response to being asked to re-brand the city, describes the place as the Original. Modern city. Susie Stubbs' paper is an engaging look at how a picture of a toaster galvanised his maverick mind and began the journey to become Creative Director of the city. It is about the journey from the disgruntled McEnroe Group (named after the tennis player's famous phrase "You cannot be serious!"), set up to petition the city council to do better with its public face, to the Manchester International Festival and beyond. Saville has always been vocal in his support for the art that makes a city, and here he talks about ways to keep the best in the region and pull in new talent at the same time.

Complimentary to Susie's article is a piece by cultural commentator Jon Savage that pinpoints the eclectic constellation of events, ideas and ideals that led to the establishment of a definitive musical identity rooted in the ginnels, alleyways and factories of the region. He looks at how a specific cultural economy selected on the basis of the formidable reputations they are forging for themselves internationally and who are cementing the region as a cornerstone of contemporary art practice. They illustrate for us the diversity of methodologies, the variety of concerns and the exciting new approaches that the fine arts are taking across the region. We garner from them their views and experiences of living along the region, and gather insight into the micro influences that brought them, keep them and inspire them along the way.

At the heart of the magazine sits a double-sided pullout. On one side Laura Mansfield has put together, with the help of Corridor8 designers Studio Dust, a snapshot, a slice in time, of some of the nebulous activities of some of the key operators in the region. This mind map of cultural activity in the

Welcome to Corridor8

Spread across and through the pages of this magazine is the concept of the city. Its restlessness pervades each line and title, each image and voice. We set out, way back at the first conception of this publication, to bring together a set of articles, people, places and ideas that actively sought, using the restless energy of city, to re-define our understanding of the loci of force that makes it what it is. These are mavericks, vanguard art practices, hard to define in-betweeners, cutting out a cave for themselves in the cultural rock face and performing their own idiosyncratic brand of city magic.

The city that we looked at is not a given and bounded place, as Iain Sinclair makes amply clear, nor is it simply the elaborate conceit of an architect, or love child of policymakers and business strategists. It is a corridor. It is a northern way, a northern island, a conduit, a corridor. It is the places camped by the water, iron and asphalt rivers. It is the region that strides from Liverpool in the east to Hull in the west, and beyond to Dublin and Denmark. It is the Transpennine region, the 'SuperCity' of Will Alsop, North as opposed to South.

Yet it is this an area that benefits from such remote definitions? How do we create parity across the regions of the country and say, without resorting to clichés, what makes a region uniquely valuable within it? What are the dynamics of a place, the idiosyncrasies of its cultural activities, the mechanics of the movement of cultural ideas across this linear cluster of settlements? Is there a conceptual thread that holds things together? How do we measure the cohesion of a region with such disparate historical divides? Is a more genuine identity subsumed by the attempt to codify a region into a coherent and identifiable place or sentiment just so that we can see it in apposition to 'the other'? This is what we are investigating here, in the pages of Corridor8.

Within these pages you will find a specially commissioned piece by writer Iain Sinclair (*Lights Out for the Territory; London Orbital*). He is our 'eyes outside'. He travels the neck of the country, east to west, then west to east, by car and then bus pass, absorbing, reflecting and critiquing with that eye turned to the minutiae of everyday life. It is the poet's eye for the human in spaces, the presence in absence. The anti-architect of the living place. His conclusions are as inspired as they are unexpected, and make a pertinent point of departure for a magazine that is setting out to look differently from the beginning. Joining him on this poetic Fear and Loathing in Las Vegas-style road grew in inverse proportion to the evaporating workplace. As penury became commonplace, what forces converged on a specific city that showed the way to get those empty hands out of pockets and send them soaring into the air? The answers came, the culture morphed and the people endured — bringing us Factory Records, The Haçienda and Tony Wilson's 24-hour memorial talkathon.

As an artist and lecturer across the region for the last forty years, and with his innovative web space projects soanyway.org.uk and slashseconds.org, Derek Horton is well placed to extend the theme of retaining creative capital in the region. He considers what a SuperCity art school might look like, imagineering an approach that harks back to the lost utopian drive of the 1960's and 70's whilst simultaneously forward to a technologically savvy 'connectedness' that utilises 21st Century tools of communication and a new approach to the concept of space. This skeletal manifesto is the bones on which everyone is invited to graft some flesh, building a beast which may just walk or waltz us into the 22nd Century.

Artist, curator and patisserie project manager Paul Bradley talks to Dan McClean about the political and artistic landscape of the region from the unstable 1970's and 80's through to the period in the 90's when West Yorkshire became the centre of international sculptural practice. In looking at the meaning of True North, we take in the Orgreave protests of the Miner's Strike, visionary monks, bin bags and radical theatre. His first patisserie project, by international artist Michelangelo Pistoletto, is featured on the front cover of this publication.

In Liverpool and Denmark Marie-Anne McQuay elaborates on how radicalised art group Superflex galvanised a community to save itself with the aid of the internet and how, under the guidance of Glasgow-born, Hull and Liverpool-based and Leeds working social provocateur and artist Alan Dunn, reached across geographical boundaries to touch others in Brazil, Thailand and Antarctica.

Laura Mansfield investigates the Salford Restoration Office who, extending the inclusive nature of art practice to include cultural institutions themselves, works across the Transpennine region and beyond, utilising the administrative and bureaucratic systems in the art world as a tool in their practice to empower (and employ) artists.

Towards the centre of this magazine we profile the work of eight emerging artists who operate along the corridor. These 'Flash Artists', as we term them, are cloud of the North is intended to give an indication of the clusters of interest (the fires that spark fires) that are constantly evolving across and beyond its borders. The health of the cloud, and its flexible topology, is critical to making the region work as a whole, and the 'connectedness' which it indicates shows too that those boundaries are not restricted to the local or even national, but extend outwards to the global landscape.

On the reverse of this map we have a unique image, *Look, stranger!*, never before published, by transmedia punk, post-punk and feminist icon Linder Sterling from her concept artwork for haute couture designer Richard Nicolls' new collection. The excitement generated by this collaboration has set the world of fashion alight, and here we present an image from her original collages for the series that, as their press release indicates, seeks to takes us to a region which is unfamiliar and challenging, where new things are possible — 'And the ironic shall lead to the mythic'.

It is this expanded notion of 'region' that Corridor8 explores. We want to see not what it was or is, but how it can be. We aim to show, with a coherent, critical mind, that the future is already being explored, and bring to the fore some of the people who are pointing the way. Not East to West, West to East, North to South or South to North, but around, across, through and beyond. There is a territory to be claimed that everyone profiled here has touched upon in some way, an evolved landscape where art, architecture, space and time are reconfigured into something new.

This is not just the charge of artists. On my regular train journey to work, a community of fellow travellers has evolved. These are people who live, work and play across the region, who come together twice a day to talk, joke and share ideas. Businesses have grown, lives have been shared, successes and failures discussed. People leave or lose jobs and move cities, fresh faces appear and a new dynamic begins, growing out of the natural inclination of people towards each other. It is this energy and trajectory that Corridor8 seeks to capture.

Art moves in times of crisis, seizing opportunities and seeing possibilities where others might despair. Innovating artists embrace instability as a time for risk-taking, a time to put into practice radical schemes and a time to strike out into unknown territory. This is the time for art praxis to flourish on the Transpennine axis. It is the time for Corridor8.

Roger McKinley

Bottom
*Living L_SuperCity (2005).
Sketch by Will Alsop.*

04 — Will Alsop's Praxis

Celebrate Everything You Normally Do: Will Alsop's Praxis

Will McLean

Will Alsop's architecture is not for those of a nervous disposition. Challenging, idiosyncratic and radically inventive it positions architecture not as a function of civic pride, but as a force that stimulates new ways of seeing 'place'.

Top
Living L, SuperCity (2005).

Middle
Living L, SuperCity (2005).

Bottom
Peckham Library, London (1999).

Left Top
(Ontario College of Art & Design, Toronto (2004).

Left Bottom
The Public, West Bromwich (2008). Photograph by Wayne Fox.

The myth of the artist

'One must work at set hours every day. One must work like a workman. Anyone who has done anything worthwhile has done that.' Henri Matisse

So how about less of the romanticism that took aspiring artist Anthony Aloysius Hancock to Paris in Galton and Simpson's film *The Rebel* (1960) and more sweeping-up, pencil sharpening and the habitual behavior of the artist that occurs between the making of stuff? Hancock's artist was actually a grafter, up before and after his day job to get some artwork made. Upon his introduction to the Paris art scene, his character was asked how he mixed his paint? "In a bucket with a big stick," he barked enthusiastically.

We are ill served by someone else's definition of the artist, and when a uniquely unimaginative government starts talking about 'creativity' you know it must be time to get on with your own personal toil, which is exactly what Will Alsop does.

Notwithstanding an aversion to the fixation of the 'gifted', there are not — or do not seem to be — many characters of the Alsopian variety currently operating in the field of architecture. This is the field where the Alsop architect of ideas is called maverick, *enfant terrible* (surely there should be a sell-by date on such a term) and generally dismissed by two-handed adjective. If there is any doubt with Alsop the architect, it is not in the extremes of his work, but where projects have been tempered through unnecessarily lengthy design process, financial concerns or doubts about a project's technological realisation. This is an architecture that does not benefit from the timidity of a nervous client. Whether in the chrysalis-like potential of the Cardiff Bay Visitor's Centre, the enjoyable social utility of Peckham Library or the elevated landing deck of Toronto's OCAD art school, Alsop continues to prove his ability to divest society with some good architectural artifact.

The architect's accoutrements

There is a wonderful photograph at the front of a monograph of architect Aldo Rossi. It shows a soft pack of un-tipped Camel cigarettes, a slightly crushed diminutive can of Coca Cola, a selection of coloured chalk pencils, an ashtray, notebook and airplane ticket stub. Whilst this maybe a somewhat contrived still life (or at least a carefully art-directed one) I have no reason not to believe that this is an accurate record of the man. In the case of Will Alsop, a similar arrangement, but different catalogue of objects might begin to tell us a lot about this highly individualistic and single-minded designer. Alsop's control of conversation is one such tool. Deployed through timing that is even-paced and non hysterical as well as syntax, gesture, physical truculence, and general body language he further extends this control through the use of the occasional 'prop'. Witness Alsop at a presentation, where the strategic 'chess-like' deployment of very specific pocket-sized accoutrement, such as his modular 'golden section' box of Benson & Hedges cigarettes, a cigarette lighter disguised as a scale model of the Cardiff Bay Visitor's Centre and/or eye-glasses, glass cases, fountain-pen, et cetera. If all this seems distracting, that may be the point; he now... has our full attention.

For Alsop, architecture is not some casual pastime or socially elevated position in the manner of the gentleman farmer, and so when the prizes are being handed around by this profession of scoundrels, do-gooders and the less-than-brilliant, he does not fit comfortably into the largely dull milieu. Peckham Library, which won Alsop the Stirling Prize in 2000, had to win the prize that year and no amount of humming and hawing could have failed to recognise a piece of transformative art in the downtown melancholy of South East London.

Generationally, it is difficult to see who his peers are, which is perhaps as it should be. A half-generation younger than Richard Rogers and Norman Foster, Alsop is arguably more interested in the technology of building-scale industry than these two behemoths of a bye-gone hi-tech aesthetic who appear to have long since given up the potential of their art. Alsop does not do too much of the same thing again and again, he gets bored too easily. At a recent lecture, Alsop discussed the logic of mentor and former employer Cedric Price's refusal to date drawings on the possible basis that you never know when or where or for whom a good idea's time has come. Alsop speculated that this may have been some glorious conceit, if so he clearly suffers from the same minor affliction, keeping as he does every notebook he has ever produced, chronologically ordered and in close proximity to his desk. These books, which date from his time as a student at the Architectural Association, are a part of Alsop's whole, and contain neat structural ideas ready for re-use, diagrams of new projects and richly illustrated painted, drawn and heavily-worked imaginings of new kinds of architecture. These books also include references to composers, inventors and unorthodox characters like architect Frederick Kiesler and scientist Wilhelm Reich — coincidentally both originally from Vienna where Alsop has been Professor of Architecture at the Technical University Vienna since 1995. The possibility that a good idea or notion might not have any specified end-date is useful here, and that by leaving the 'case open' (in detective literary parlance) who knows where or when the time will come for careful deployment of such ideas? So it goes with Alsop, he is not repeating himself, but may finally get a good idea out of his system through the realisation of a project as in Peckham Library, which arguably begun with the designs for an elevated Vierendeel palace of books in Swansea, kiboshed by political temerity.

Lunch at the office

A pork pie, quartered tomatoes and English mustard.

The regulation Alsop office lunch includes a couple of regional delicacies, but moreover encapsulates a highly ritualised behaviour. Sitting in the glass prow of a former office perched at the end of Albert Bridge on the River Thames, Alsop would lunch in this goldfish bowl inviting in various staff to unpick projects, start again, remake, remodel, et cetera. Bored by the end result of some design development or engineering solution, a whole project might be re-written. As infuriating as this may be for any employee divested of some recent hard graft, this is as it should be — client or no client. And it may be that clients have been pushed away by a radical design change or a difficult idea. If architects are indeed the servants of society then they would do well as to not dish out half-baked aggregations of old ideas and highly developed concoctions of no ideas at all. If Alsop is his own worst enemy by nixing certain jobs before they even begin, then we should all be thankful.

Before we finish lunch it might be useful to mention that a good deal of early Alsop projects included the utility of the hydroponic tomato farm, and that long before the eco-trappings of gratuitous vertical greening, Alsop was thinking about both the health of the building environment and the health and nourishment of its inhabitants. His *Cologne Media Park* (1987) is a good example of the tomato farm feature and which also included a 500m-long brine pool, just wide enough to let two swimmers pass each other. Alsop's interest in aviaries (and their regular inclusion in early projects) is similarly borne out of a belief that the physical backdrop that may be provided by the architect should be at the very least physiologically and socially expansive. ▶

The drive-by site visit

'The 'client' is a combination of all who are in any way affected by the architect's action.' Cedric Price (1967)

I would like to think that Will Alsop's idealised site visit would involve a large car, let's say a Jaguar, nothing too sporty, but a serious piece of Midlands' automotive engineering moving at speed on a decent sized road past the said site. Now I would not like to suggest that he is disinclined to get his hands dirty with the physical location of some future confection, it's just that this boot-dirtying sojourn is precisely the kind of 'experience' which may prevent him thinking he can do anything at all. Set this trait against the kind of mass-involvement planning processes of his own invention in cities and towns across the Midlands and the North of England and you may have mixed messages about this architect's ability or desire to accumulate local knowledge. This is because Alsop is happy to let other members of the design team explore the physical actuality of the site for him. He has got other work to do, which involves much larger groups of people. The large-scale planning workshops, which share similarities with the Hamburg Bau-forums of the 1980's, in which Alsop participated, are not the lazy rigmaroles of drawings, models and evaded questions until home time. This is a participatory series of events to coax out themes, objects, problems and new possibilities.

An elegant extrusion

Alsop once cited *The Sea and Ships Pavilion,* Basil Spence's project for the Festival of Britain (1951), as an influence. This steel-framed open shed acted as an armature for its contents; a kind of prototypical theatrical rig, which in Spence's design contained the sheared aft-sections of several large ships. The nautical connection is relevant: large single object buildings designed in cross-section, propped up, cantilevered ... this sounds a lot like Will Alsop's work from the late 1980's and early 1990's, which included a semi-submersible river vessel several kilometers long containing such delights as a high-tide disco, a supermarket, billboard sails and light-responsive mechanical flowers. Located at Port de la Lune, Bordeaux, the *Garonne Activator* (1990) is precisely the right mix of far-out engineering, transmutable programming and time dependant delight that Alsop does so well.

On site

In the cyclical loop in which social design seems to operate, it turns out that Alsop's newfound interest in the design of bars is not so new at all. In 1985 he was engaged by proto-landlord Bill Hutcheson to re-design the interior of the forlorn Eagle pub in Farringdon Road long before the prefix 'gastro' was attached to anything other than stomach-related ailments. Alsop's plans were ambitious; I suspect the budget was less so. The design included a high-rise canopy of steel, leaf-shaped tables with accompanying precipitous bar stools bolted to the floor, which enabled the seated and mooching/leaning clientèle to share a common eye-level. The bar looked great with some re-purposed industrial chic apropos of the time, which included durbar steel chequer plate table-tops, Sottsassian zebra-striped table supports/masts, with any transitional wanting coated in a good scrim of Hammerite paint. The other big innovation was that the food was not the industrialised re-heats of the 'ye olde fayre' variety, but the novelty of freshly cooked food.

What happened? Well it was shut in six months, with Hutcheson moving on to run a number of highly successful pubs, and Alsop to become an internationally recognised architect. So what was the problem? Was it the sternum-spearing plate-steel table-leaf tips, the too-good-to-be true food? Who knows? The pub reopened with the knicky-knack gastro trappings of worn ecclesiastical chairs, clapped-out sofas and 'disinterested with attitude' service that has launched a thousand replica over-priced refreshment facilities.

Alsop's exhibit at *A&M — Department of Proper Behaviour,* with Bruce McLean and Bep Gomilla, at Valencia's Biennale 2003, refreshed this model with a more perfectly ephemeral bar, not designed to last, but to create an environment where the performance of the perfectly timed drink and the carefully placed snack (a sausage in this case) create a theatre of mannerism, gesture and performance in what Alsop would say is a "celebration of everything you normally do".

The job

Every so often, serendipity delivers a project so perfectly poised and full of potential that you could have not possibly invented it yourself. When Bernard Tschumi described winning the Parc de Villette project in Paris, he said that it was as if everything he had worked at previously was somehow in preparation for that moment. In 1993, Australian artist Arthur Boyd had gifted Australia his Bundanon home, and invited Alsop to create a new arts foundation in Shoalhaven, New South Wales. Boyd had asked Alsop to... "Make a landscape into a possible container for a vision that is concerned with unknown behaviour".

Alsop had visited the site, met Boyd and came back with two books of drawings. Along with the heavily worked painted pages of Alsop's increasingly large notebooks, there were diagrams and workings in ink of a series of 'rocks'. Numbering ten in all, Alsop proposed to scatter objects, social function and amenity across the artist's 'garden'. I was a member of the office at the time and was charged with assisting architect and exquisite draughtsman Jonathan Adams. We set about producing architectural perspectives in coloured lead on tracing paper, at precisely the moment that the office's transition from analogue to digital drawing was taking place. This may all have been a huge folly — and we were indeed designing huge follies — but this was architecture, making something out of nothing, an intellectual and metaphysical investiture that can crystallise into 'actual' stuff.

The rocks were an inventory of Alsopian conceits, part Priceian magic, and part tripped-out-prog-rock fables, all with a good measure of engineering invention. The Bundanon Rocks included delights like the talking rock, the dreaming rock, the dancing rock, and the opera rock, and apparatus such as a platform for a conversation (formerly known as a table) and the store, which also acted as a man-made hill with WCs inside. Alsop's use of language, and the manner in which projects are named and described, is a very useful tool in the development of the unknown. Borrowed from Cedric Price and Buckminster Fuller, the linguistic possibility of some oddly titled project may indeed sufficiently intrigue or excite those in and around a scheme to believe in its actualisation.

Boots and shoes

That Alsop had the courage to take on re-planning Northampton to include a fledgling boot and shoe museum, a kilometer-long art park and numerous inhabited bridges, was not a mystery, as he certainly has the qualifications. A local boy, he was brought up on the Bassett-Lowke-sponsored architectural treasures of a Charles Rennie Macintosh house and the proto-modernity of Peter Behrens's New Ways house, both tucked away in and around the shoe-making capital of Britain. You should be aware, though, that this is a man who has been spotted wearing white shoes and, make no mistake, this is no Goodyear-welted architectural esthete we are talking about here. This is a person for whom the po-faced peddlers of the shadow-gap fraternity do not qualify as architects. Denude away, but will there be anything left when what Alsop calls the boring architects are finished sharpening their folksy pencils? In an unseemly display of hubris, it seemed his fellow architects were only too keen to get their well-shod boots into Liverpool's Fourth Grace project, calling for the end of iconic architecture, lumping-in Alsop with Gehry and anything vaguely exuberant, and ushering in a new age of... what, precisely? An architecture of boredom perhaps? Acres of limestone floors, where the last expression of *jeux de vie* is the multi-coloured reception desk... it does not have to be like this.

Now

So what now? Well, the routines continue, they slightly change, they always include students (currently in Vienna), new projects, new associations and the assistance of right-hand men Tim Thornton and George Wade for the enlightened use of digital tools. With the communication of ideas increasingly relayed through filmmaking and animation, there is close collaboration with son Oliver's Squint Opera Company.

Projects like SuperCity started to go beyond the waiting-for-the-phone-to-ring modus operandi of the contemporary professional architect. Not waiting to be asked, Alsop proceeds with ambitious plans for a massive area traversing the country between Liverpool and Hull. Recently re-visiting this project with the specific utility of the liquid refreshment 'bar' facility, Alsop begins to explore how a knitted-together North of England might feel like in his speculative 'satellite towns' project. Alsop asks what is it about new settlements that is important or missing, and suggests myth and ritual as key components to sustain our desire to be in a place, with the bar (or inn) operating as the social stage or condenser for stories of past and future adventures. Add to this Alsop's suggestion that the physical moving of earth may also give shape to useful points of reference, such as the hill or pond, and these new living places begin to develop sufficient complexity to sustain their existence. As with Cedric Price's Potteries *Thinkbelt* project the ambition of any given project need not be limited by previous assumption.

The generalist schooling of the architect is rarely celebrated. Richard Buckminster Fuller recognised it's potential, as did the cyberneticist Gordon Pask, who saw a very useful shared set of systems thinking. Cedric Price was one of the few 20th Century architects to actually practice in this expanded field. William Alsop is a part of this tradition, and equally has created his own world of architecture. "No style, no beauty," he says. This is not to deny either, but to countenance the notion of architecture extending its commodity into the realm of the idea, the social, that of reading a book, making a painting, having a swim and enjoying a drink, cantilevered out over some extraordinary environment and afforded a good measurement of generosity by a remarkable architect.

Will McLean runs 'McLean's Nuggets' in Architectural Design magazine. He is Senior Lecturer in the School of Architecture and the Built Environment at the University of Westminster.

Top Left
The Beauty Department, Department Store of Proper Behaviour, Valencia (2003).

Top Right
The Drinking Department, Department Store of Proper Behaviour, Valencia (2003).

Middle
Posing Structure, Department Store of Proper Behaviour, Valencia (2003).

Bottom
Infrastructure Village, SuperCity (2005).

07 — Will Alsop's Praxis

Top
I Wish My Garden Was Really Like This (2009). Acrylic on canvas.

Bottom
Cultural fog at the Olga Korper Gallery, Toronto (2007). 150 x 120cm.

08 – Sensual Cities

Sensual Cities

Phil Griffin

Will Alsop's credibility as an architect is undoubted. Yet increasingly he is being recognised for his other practice, in the less visible and more humble form as a painter. What is it then that keeps pulling him back to this more intimate act and how does this feed his passion for creating living spaces? To throw light on this double life Phil Griffin asks the question: Is he an architect who paints, or a painter who makes buildings?

Painting is a way of ordering the world. Whether it delivers a version of Creation, the hierarchy of the Spanish royal household, domestic life in 17th Century Delft, or the aftermath of an air raid, a painting — be it as seeming-literal as George Stubbs or as abstract as Jackson Pollock — is an organisation of what is, or is imagined to be. When Yves Klein descended on his IKB — International Klein Blue — and decided that all his monochrome paintings would be that same colour, he so refined the world as almost to own a slice of the spectrum. He signed the sky.

Understandably, painting has its attractions to architects. There may be a lot of things going on in the head of an architect, but order is the controlling factor. One architect of my acquaintance will tidy the entire pub — beer-mats, crisp packets and all — before settling down with his pint (he was a nightmare before the smoking ban). Another changes seats in Starbuck's half a dozen times before draining his cappuccino.[1] They do these things, these organisers of windows, doors and ways we are supposed to live.

Will Alsop paints; usually in acrylic, often on large canvases loosely attached to walls. His paintings are expressive, colourful, and their relationship with his architecture is pretty clear. Alsop's paintings are the sketchbooks of a man who is like an architect, only bigger. Unusually for an architect in the present day, Alsop uses colour confidently and well. With a few notable exceptions (Sauerbruch Hutton, say) most architects are poor colourists.[2] Alsop is especially good at wheeling a trolley-full of acrylic squeeze bottles around a problem.

He is also an architect who takes photos, writes, reads, and gardens and hunts truffles. I know of one successful architect (I might have mentioned him before) whose only reading is Classic Car Magazine, which would at least have given him something to chat with Corbusier about. Alsop, on the other hand, is a culture botherer. He even goes to the opera.

Painting is on the up. (I think you could) Put this down to three Gerhard Richter exhibitions in the UK within the last twelve months. The 2009 Turner Prize shortlist comprises four people who may actually, from time-to-time, use paint.

Bottom
Cultural fog at the Olga Korper Gallery, Toronto (2007). 150 x 120cm.

Below
Will Alsop & Bruce McLean, Malagarba (1999).

Top, Middle & Bottom
Cultural fog at the Olga Korper Gallery, Toronto (2007). 150 x 120cm.

10 — Sensual Cities

People enjoy the paintings of Peter Doig. On 14th October 2007 a painting of his called *Concrete Cabin* (1991-92) sold at Christie's for £916,500. It is one of a series based on Le Corbusier's *Unite D'Habitation*. Not the celebrated building in Marseilles, but the one in Briey-en-Forêt, Northern France. The one built in 1961 and abandoned and derelict by 1973.

Doig says, "When I went to see the Le Corbusier building for the first time, I never dreamed that I would end up painting it. I went for a walk in the woods on one visit, and as I was walking back I suddenly saw the building anew. I had no desire to paint it on its own, but seeing it through the trees, that is when I found it striking." Peter Doig approaches a building and makes a painting. Will Alsop makes a painting and approaches a building.

In early summer 2007 Will Alsop showed at the Olga Korper Gallery in Toronto. The show was called Cultural View and comprised a dozen or so pictures, 53.5 by 65.5 cm, mixed media on paper. The work was generated by an architectural project to redevelop Kensington Market. Much of it puts me in mind of Doig's *Concrete Cabin* series. Both bodies of work scatter architectural forms behind dense chaotic overlay. Both sequences have great depth without resort to formal perspective. Both manipulate the journey through the frame by carefully positioned reds, whites and high-points.

Professor William Alsop OBE RA is co-curator of the Royal Academy Summer Exhibition 2009. That's a very 19th Century thing for an avant-garde architect to be doing. Despite tabletop multi-coloured rakish iconoclastic buildings, Alsop is an unreconstructed cultural toff. A Clerkenwell Ranger (whose Studio is in Battersea). Flâneur. Tippler. Dandy. Lizard. Alsop is a *joyeuse* addict. An organ for the reception of pleasures. Lucky for some that his hedonism is tethered to the architect's control urges. Lucky for those he lives and works with. Alsop's route to the building, cabin, academy, library, department store, is down backstreets, past the sex museum, through the bar. The city of the senses. His CV includes years teaching sculpture at Central St Martin's. If someone had bought him a fiddle, I guess he might have spent time at Guildhall.

Alsop has a long relationship with Professor Bruce McLean, Head of Graduate Painting at the Slade.[3] Together they are a knock-about duo. McLean can don the dark suit of opening nights, and Alsop crook his little finger by the Merlot of the audience q & a, but really they'd much prefer to be back at the beginning, standing in the field of big nothing in which something has to happen.

In early summer 2002 the field was in Malagarba, central Menorca, a farm McLean has had a number of years. The two men habitually work this space, exploring mental annexes and pitched tents of their own invention. Setting up possibilities. Posing in sunshine. The art, on these occasions, is mixed media. There are painted 3D constructions, and bright self-coloured surfaces, which escape the farmyard and skitter around the fields, free-range. There might be a launch pad, such as an architectural competition or a gallery commission that throws the two men, and their family helpers, into creative frenzy. Carnival work, like a float or tableau for a Menorcan festival. *Malagarba Works*[4] lead to exhibitions in Milton Keynes and Manchester. These were never going to be sombre affairs.

The point of the work always seemed to me the mood it communicated; of freedom and fun, surprise and life affirmation. With regard to Alsop, this cuts to the problem that some have with his architecture; it is so damned upbeat. Frivolous, some would say; throwaway, trivial, ephemeral, lacking gravitas, lacking an 'ism', messy, garish, lumpy, attention seeking, wilful, silly. Peckham Library, Toronto College of Art and Design, Chips New Islington; these are unmistakably Alsop buildings and they are the ones which most relate to his painting. These are fundamental Alsop buildings put together by paintbrush, palette knife and squeegee. In other, comparably unshackled, skittish architectural hands, they might have been folded card, sliced polystyrene, balsa or vinyl. Playful media. Skills, thrills, frills and craft. If you want another architecture, look elsewhere. If you want the polite modernism of sequential fenestration, symmetry, reverent context and miles of shadow gap, look away now.

In 2003 Alsop produced the master plan for New Islington, a designated Millennium Community[5] just east of Manchester city centre. The council-owned land, and low-lying Seventies housing estate that leached across it, squatted between the Rochdale and Ashton canals. Alsop painted them out. He swept a blue arch connecting the waterways. He brushed out the dead-end streets and misproportioned spaces and stroked-in a handful of wharves and thousands of metres of waterfront. His painting described a watery bridge between the two canals. A water-park beside the city's ring road. Islands, reed beds, pontoons and urban barns. He painted a new order, and curved his Chips building down the Ashton canal towpath. He reproduced his painting in inks on a white board in a contractor's production office later in the process. Except the 'white board' turned out to be an expensive projection screen. Nobody had the nerve to stop him. It's probably still there.

The painter Gerhard Richter is the architect of many of his own exhibitions. Also, he designed his own house. He says,[6] "Architecture was, or is, a kind of hobby, an inclination I have to fiddling around and building things... If social changes are in the air, I am gripped immediately by the desire to build... In the case of my house, that was anticipation: in other words, first build, then change one's life." His is a useful antidote to Alsop. The architect deals in social change, in so far as a new and architecturally outspoken library, say, is a catalyst or herald of change. For Alsop painting is the foreground activity, the mechanism by which he can order space: in other words, first paint, then change people's lives. Hopefully, for better, and without resort to doctrine or autocracy.

Alsop and McLean's Malagarba Works are clear indication that the two men will someday create great opera or ballet sets.[7] Their work together at Riverside Studios in the late 1970's probably set up the same possibilities. They are gregarious men who welcome collaborators, providing potential fellow workers are firmly in their thrall. Alsop is a studio man. He once told me he needs people around he can steal ideas from. For him painting is clearly the medium of sequestration. In painting he rubs colour against colour, piles form on form, inter-cuts dimensions expands the ground. He does things that are architectural and discovers resolutions and solutions, which he would not arrive at by any better means. To build a set, platform, box, frame or arch, and then to place objects, natural or fabricated in it, is place-making. It is also painting. What sets Will Alsop aside from most other architects is that he paints to build. He has, and always has had, a painter's eye. His is not the only way to make buildings, but it is egregiously and humanely his way. And (like them or not) his buildings are uniquely engaging.

Phil Griffin is a writer and broadcaster with special interest in architecture and urban development. He was born in Ancoats, Manchester, on the site of Will Alsop's masterplan for New Islington.

[1] *Also, on seeing a magpie he automatically makes a two fingered salute and chants, "Good morning Mr Magpie, how are you today?" He is, I must point out, an astonishingly successful architect, which makes me wonder at the power of magpies.*

[2] *More's the pity, since the liberal use of freehand colour was never more inviting. Back-painted, screen-printed, film-backed, sandblasted, acid-etched glass is all available. There is a small school of architects who sign themselves in powder-painted panels of Rietveld colours. They often wear bright cashmere scarves in winter.*

[3] *Bruce's son is Willy McLean. His dad was a Glasgow architect, who was ambitious for his son to take on the practice. Architecture skipped a generation. I blame the Sixties.*

[4] *Malagarba Works, Bruce McLean & William Alsop, Wiley-Academy, 2002.*

[5] *New Islington used to be called the Cardroom Estate. It is 25 acres (10 hectares) just outside Manchester's inner ring road. The area is Ancoats, and it is on the margins of the world's first industrial suburb. The lead developer is Urban Splash, doyen of contemporary apartment living. It contains Alsop's only residential block, Chips, completed in summer 2009. Sadly, due to the downturn, not much else will happen at New Islington for the foreseeable future.*

[6] *Quoted in Gerhard Richter TEXT, Thames & Hudson, 2009 (p 519).*

[7] *Bruce McLean once auditioned for Ballet Rambert. In 1971 he formed Nice Style, "The world's first pose band". He has never quite given up on the ambition.*

Right Top
Will Alsop & Bruce McLean, Malagarba (2002).

Right Bottom
Will Alsop & Bruce McLean, Malagarba (1999).

11 — Sensual Cities

12 — Palm-fringed disco

Palm-fringed disco: Peter Saville

Susie Stubbs

Peter Saville's appointment to be Manchester's Creative Director was a bold and, some would say, inevitable move that sent a message to the world that the city was finally ready to enter modern cultural life. Susie Stubbs talks to him about the trajectory that brought his curve-ball ideas back into the fold and how the Original Modern concept is taking its effect.

Photograph courtesy Anna Blessman.

Peter Saville is one of Manchester's greatest creative exports. This is the seminal designer who, having cut his teeth at Factory Records, went on to change the face of British design; a man whose influence stretches from the YBAs to the iPod, a creative talent whose clients include Roxy Music, Yohji Yamamoto and the Centre Pompidou. And yet, having travelled so far during the course of a career that spans three decades, Peter Saville has come home. He is back in Manchester, the architect of its recent branding exercise, the champion of Mancunian wit, intelligence and innovation. "I am a local boy with some visionary qualities," says Saville, by way of explanation. "Because of Tony Wilson, I was able to do something with those qualities when I was young. Because of Factory Records, I had an opportunity that turned out to be of enormous significance." Saville pauses for a moment. "There is something very beautiful whereby twenty-five years later the city itself asks me to do for it what I had done for Factory."

On paper, it had looked persuasively simple. Manchester, a city that had for years toiled to extricate itself from the post-industrial mire, wanted to ensure that a more favourable light was shone upon it. Despite the shiny new galleries that stretched from the Ship Canal to the city centre; the footballers gazing out of the windows of their penthouses; the financial institutions jostling to open regional HQs; despite even the success of the Commonwealth Games, Manchester was still portrayed by some as a parochial, irrelevant town. But Manchester was nothing if not ambitious: it wanted to compete not with London but with Milan, Frankfurt, Barcelona. As Sir Howard Bernstein, Chief Executive of the City Council, said of the Commonwealth Games in 2002, "This is what I call maybe stage two of about ten years' hard work, the aim of which was to make us a very successful regional capital. Once the Games have finished we can then really strike out."

To help in that striking out, Manchester called on one of its own, appointing Saville as its Creative Director and asking him to build a visual identity for the city that would change its fortunes (or at least its national and international profile). In many ways, it made perfect sense. Saville has an almost mythical status within the design world, and his credibility was crucial in ensuring the project was a political success because, when it came to destination branding, Manchester had form. In 1997, in the aftermath of the IRA bomb, Marketing Manchester came up with a strapline for the city that trumpeted, 'We're up and going'. The implication, that Manchester was a plucky little place just about managing to pull itself up by its bootstraps, had few fans. Tony Wilson and friends formed the McEnroe Group (their slogan, 'you cannot be serious'), and swiftly dismissed the effort as 'mediocrity at its most mediocre'. The campaign was quietly dropped and, ten years later, when the city felt strong enough to brave a similar exercise, Tony Wilson et al were invited to suggest who might be the best man for the job. There was only ever one real candidate: Saville.

Despite the near universal support for Saville's appointment, however, it was never going to be a straightforward job. For a start, Saville baulks at the notion that he is 'just' a graphic designer. This is a man, after all, who has spent his considerable creative talents meditating on the subject of communication, who has taken the lessons of Modernism and delivered them, to a mass audience, via the channels of pop culture. Graphic design, to Saville, is just one part of an aesthetic puzzle that spans disciplines as diverse as advertising, music, fashion, industrial and product design, photography, regeneration, economics and fine art. So while the Manchester job may have been a commercial contract, part of its appeal lay beyond remuneration: it was rooted in Saville's fascination in the interplay between art and life and, as a result, there was always going to be a gap between the client's expectations and the product that Saville eventually delivered. There was something else, too, that Saville believes was never fully understood by his new patrons. Manchester failed to appreciate Factory's cultural significance, to comprehend what Factory did — and, in many ways, still does — for the city. "The fact that Manchester hasn't yet fully understood that something that so influenced the modern world came from the city is a bit frustrating," he says. "There was a reason why the artists who got involved in Manchester International Festival did so, and that reason is related to Factory and the Haçienda and their deep sense of respect for both. And yet the Haçienda has gone, there is no formal recognition of Factory anywhere, and there should be because it forms the contemporary cultural provenance of the city.

"What a city does and makes is fundamental to what it communicates," he continues. "If I had been commissioned by Liverpool and we looked at the Beatles, I would ask, does the city, intellectually, understand the importance of the Beatles? The answer is, no. But, by coincidence, because this is Manchester, I have to suggest that the city doesn't understand Factory. The real importance of it they haven't even started on." For its part, the city remains indifferent. The Haçienda was pulled down and there is no sign that anyone wants to re-build it. In its place sits a characterless apartment block, one whose identikit flats were sold with the strapline, 'Now the party's over, it's time to come home'. Neat line, but the party was never the point. The Haçienda was about more than acid house. It was about more than raves and drugs and police raids. The Haçienda was the centre of something that, even now, remains hard to define: it was the place or the point at which a set of disparate individuals, pulled into Tony Wilson's stellar orbit, were given the opportunity to re-imagine their city.

"The young and romantic always leave to go to the place where their romantic vision draws them and, for one reason, Tony basically, a group of people chose to stay and change their here and now," says Saville. "And they changed Manchester. The city is still living on the reverberation of that. Factory, the Haçienda, Joy Division, New Order: they changed the understanding of popular culture in Britain. And, critically, the Haçienda suggested there might be a point to this former industrial city. It did that because Ben Kelly took the DNA of the city and reconstituted it into the now. The Haçienda was not some palm-fringed fucking disco. It took the industrial aesthetic and reconstituted it, and the point was that it was the child of the industrial city and it suggested that there may be a conceptual future for such a place." Yet although Saville argues that the city has little awareness of what the Haçienda did, not just for Manchester but for post-industrial centres across the world, there is some level of understanding; there is the desire, at least, that the city reinvent itself once more, this time not as a subterranean hub of youth culture but as a 21st Century, European city. Manchester, like Saville, has grown up; what the city appears to struggle with is to articulate how it got there and where, exactly, it has to go next.

As Saville began work, the gulf between what the city expected and Saville's thinking, widened. Saville knew that the city didn't need a proper, old-fashioned, made-in-the-1950's-when-advertising-still-worked campaign: a logo, a strapline, perhaps a series of glossy ads. It didn't need one; Saville argued that no amount of adverts in newspaper supplements would change people's view of Manchester. Instead, he focused on an intellectual repositioning of the city, in a form of communication that, by escaping the confines of branding, could unleash something far more meaningful — one that could, realistically, change some of those hard to shift perceptions.

Left
Lighting installations 1 & 2 erected in a tunnel used by attendees of the Labour Party Conference, Manchester 2006, behind Manchester Central conference and exhibition centre. The Labour Party's AGM had not been held in Manchester for almost 100 years. Photography courtesy Steve Connor / Creative Concern www.creativeconcern.com Installations by Creative Concern / Peter Saville.

13 — Palm-fringed disco

The roots of this thinking can be traced back to 1970's Manchester. As a student at the then Polytechnic, Saville discovered, in a book borrowed from the library, Richard Hamilton's *Toaster,* a beautifully crafted piece of Pop art that fuses product design and fine art — and which had an enormous impact on the young Saville. He didn't see the work again until the turn of this century but, when he did, Saville saw his entire body of work in it. "It really unsettled me. What I had taken from it was that there was a co-ordinate point between all of the disciplines: industrial design, photography, graphics, typography and fine art; there was a kind of utopian co-ordinate point where our æsthetic awareness is able to come together in a single work." *Toaster* is highly seductive. It shows a version of post-war life where art and the everyday are unified, where mass production hasn't led to an erosion of quality (of life, of the products we buy) but instead enhanced it. "It suggested to me that the things we produce as part of our everyday experience can benefit from the things we've learned so far. Why does there have to be a compromise, why is there a division between art and life? It led me towards a cursive point between art and life and that is a point of view I pretty much still hold."

It's clear that Saville, even while still at college, began to look beyond the discipline he was being taught. "I ignored graphics. I was completely out of sync with the prevailing school of thought in communications design. I found it banal. I didn't need such simplistic forms of communication because I was looking at image and lifestyle and the convergent points of culture and life." It is little wonder, then, that Saville was not content to simply bang out a visual identity for Manchester and move on. The city, however, was expecting a new brand — although those expectations should come as no great surprise. We live in a society that, overwhelmed by an endless stream of information (visual, corporate, textual, audio), no longer has time for considered detail. As Robert Hughes wrote in *The Shock of the New*, 'There is no way of paying equal attention to all that surplus, so we skim. The image we remember is the one that most resembles a sign: simple, clear, repetitious.' We are in thrall to the 'tyranny of branding', as Saville puts it, where the cult of celebrity is in the ascendant and where ordinary people have themselves become brands. Saville is one such brand — the mythology around both him and Factory is one reason why he got the Manchester gig. So if we can turn people into products, why shouldn't we also make a commodity of the city?

The trouble is that branding of this nature is often superficial. The cities that have embarked on similar self-branding exercises tend to say the same thing: they declare themselves dynamic, exciting, cutting-edge, world class. The terms are interchangeable. The descriptions could be peeled off and swapped around and no one would be any the wiser. The tyranny of visual branding has created dull, homogenous cities — at least in terms of how they are developed, packaged and sold to the outside world. And the one thing that Manchester should never be accused of is being dull.

So Saville didn't deliver a brand. Instead, he came up with a 'brand vision': the argument that Manchester is the Original Modern city. The reasoning followed thus: if Manchester collectively aspired to be original and modern in what it did, it would not only have a brand, it would be a brand. It could build on its reputation as a city of 'firsts', the cradle of the industrial revolution, the birthplace of the computer and test-tube babies, all of that, without forever looking over its shoulder. It could use the Original Modern concept to turn its face to the future. It was a simple repositioning of the world's first industrial city. And yet — it wasn't what anyone had expected. "People didn't get it immediately and there is probably just a small number of people who get it now," says Nick Johnson, Deputy Chief Executive of property development firm, Urban Splash. "I had the Chamber of Commerce telling me they didn't know what it meant; that it felt a bit like the Emperor's New Clothes." Others took it a little too literally: a glut of organisations, universities, club nights, even a radio station (BBC Radio Manchester, for the record), labelled themselves 'original and modern' – and, in doing so, completely missed the point. Original Modern is not an easy solution to Manchester's ills. It is not a strapline that can be applied to a sub-standard product to make it better, and Saville readily admits to disappointment at the number of people who think that it is. "Original Modern is not a sound bite, it is a challenge that says to be original and modern there are things that you have to do," he says. "It can be expressed through transport, architecture, education — whatever, it doesn't matter, it is an attitude appropriate to the provenance of the city, and we can pursue it anywhere."

Four years into the campaign, and the city's uptake of the Original Modern vision is only now beginning to grow. Johnson refers to Original Modern as 'a clarion call' and yet confesses that it has been difficult to communicate exactly what it means to the city at large. "As soon as I heard the phrase, I understood its resonance and potential," he says. "I positioned it as an economic development strategy, partly to rebuff those who considered it to be a strapline or a logo or a piece of copywriting — by doing so, it became a provocation for people to think about the city in a different way. It means that if every business in the region asks themselves whether they are being original and modern, and adjusts their horizons accordingly, then they will improve the cultural and economic output of the region immeasurably."

Saville himself vacillates between frustration and acceptance of Manchester's reaction to his work. "Tony thought I would become a muse to Sir Howard Bernstein in the way I had been to him. The reality, of course, wasn't like that. Factory afforded me carte blanche to do anything and in any way. There were no experienced gatekeepers, no managers or promoters and no investors. No capital was involved, so no one was answerable to anyone," he says. "Tony didn't tell me to do anything but he was interested in why I did what I did. This was the Factory principle throughout. Factory created opportunity." Manchester City Council isn't Factory Records, and Wilson had a freedom that the Town Hall doesn't: the space to let his artists get on with their thing without having to worry unduly about the end result. It paid off. It led to Peter Saville's iconic design; it underpinned the music of Joy Division, New Order and the Happy Mondays. But that level of uncertainty, the fact that you can never be sure what you'll end up with (if anything), is hard to justify once you open the public purse. In the public sector it's all about outcomes, boxes ticked and a careful, quantifiable measurement of the effectiveness of spending — the "metric channels of the public sector", to quote Saville. In such an environment, is it any wonder that it has taken this long to adjust to what is essentially the antithesis of a brand — particularly when what had been commissioned was meant to be brand development?

Today, Saville continues to call for an engagement with the issues that need to be tackled if Manchester is to fulfil its promise as the original, modern city. "The ideas that are needed to stimulate and drive economic development in Manchester are fed by culture," he says. "This is something the political sector doesn't fully appreciate: they think that the people who are key to economic regeneration just sit at computers and knock out ideas. It's not that simple, and the paucity of culture here is a brake on mature development. You can inspire young people, certainly. Between sixteen and eighteen you can rail at the world from your unformed perspective, you can be creatively angry at the world from a background of nothing. But beyond that you need ideas, information and education. Bands come out of places like Manchester, but where are the artists, the writers, the entrepreneurs? Where is the next level? They move on. Therefore it's critical, if we are to keep progressive, ambitious people in the city, to create the right kind of intellectual environment."

Last summer, in the aftermath of Tony Wilson's death, Saville proposed that the city stage a twenty-four hour "intelligent conversation". Over the course of a day and a night, some of Manchester's best-known artists, musicians, actors, writers and more talked to two hundred of the city's emerging artists. The Tony Wilson Experience was perhaps an attempt to create the kind of Haçienda-like space that would afford young people the opportunity to learn, debate, question, theorise and think — to create the kind of "intellectual environment" that would keep them in Manchester, rather than have them drift off to the bright lights of Paris, Berlin or New York. And it did mark a change in attitude. Chaotic and experimental (it was dubbed "shambolic enough to be useful" by one of the participants), the Tony Wilson Experience would have been unthinkable only a few years ago. Before Saville's appointment, Wilson would probably have been honoured with a plaque and a nice civic lunch.

Elsewhere, Saville speaks of the appointment of Alex Poots, the Director of Manchester International Festival, as "a great success". The festival is perhaps the most singular attempt by the City Council to create a space for Manchester at the global cultural table, with Poots taking the city's musical heritage and history of innovation and re-working both into a contemporary and defiantly Mancunian product. With a slew of international artists, a deliberate merging of creative disciplines and over twenty new commissions, the festival is doing much to shift perceptions. Its artists appear beguiled by the city: Jeremy Deller, the Turner Prize-winning artist whose commission is to be premiered in 2009, said at its launch, "For me, for some time, all roads have been leading to Manchester. I have been so inspired by the industrial and, more recently, the musical history of the town." The Observer critic, Miranda Sawyer, declared the first festival a "... real event. Britain may be awash with arts festivals — Glastonbury, Edinburgh, Hay, the Proms — but the Mancunian effort feels unique."

Attitudes are shifting beyond the arts. In 2006, the Labour Party held its first annual conference in Manchester for almost a century; 2009 sees the Tories chasing votes by staging their first major conference here, too. Saville's work alone cannot be responsible for enticing politicians from London en masse, but it does play a part in Manchester's ongoing reinvention. "Original Modern grasps the profound history of this city and suggests an inherent desire to innovate and be original," says Nick Johnson. "Therefore, what Peter has done is to distil some incredibly complex notions of culture and economics into a popular and accessible reduction. It's what he has done throughout his career — made subjects accessible without belittling their intellectual endeavour — and that's what Original Modern does.'

Twenty-five years on from Factory, four years in to its self-styled status as the Original Modern city, what does Manchester look like? Those at the top of the local political tree call it 'a city in progress', and it is: remarkable in parts, this is a city that nevertheless has much ground to cover. Sections of its economy still

Below
*Toaster (1967).
Richard Hamilton
© Richard Hamilton.
All Rights Reserved,
DACS 2009.
©Tate, London 2009.*

struggle, while some of its communities, particularly in the north, are among the poorest in Europe. It still rains, and Manchester is very far from being the architecturally coherent metropolis of its post-war dreams. Yet people still come here. The mythology of Factory lingers on, despite the indifference of the city that created it. Saville argues that Factory Records democratised urban culture — it gave young people the chance to participate in "entry-level high culture", as he puts it. Factory gave people — whether they were from Manchester or not, whether they were posh kids from the suburbs or working-class lads from Salford — the chance to be part of something. It created a sense of opportunity, and that sense, intangible though it might be, half-hidden by the new shops and apartments that sprang up during the boom: that sense of creative opportunity still, resonates. It could be that, simply because it is so intangible, the city struggles to articulate it. It could be that, because there's nothing on the street, no museum or marker to flag up its importance, those young creatives who come here now, and have no overt interest in Factory or haven't studied the canon of art and design as Saville sees it, aren't fully aware of it. But as the recession tightens its grip and begins to strangle the breath from an economy that only ever teetered on the precipice of toxic debt, perhaps this sense of opportunity will grow. After all, Manchester in the 1970's and 80's provided the most fertile of soil for a counter-culture that would change the city's fortunes for the next three decades. Manchester in the first recession of the 21st Century: maybe this, too, will become a place blooming with ideas and radical thought rather than simply booming with apartments and office blocks.

Maybe that is what keeps Saville, a local boy with 'visionary qualities', coming back. And with Original Modern acting as a roadmap, maybe this is what makes Manchester more than it ever should be: the sense of opportunity, the feeling of freedom, the space to ask questions and, sometimes, for the world to listen to the answers.

Susie Stubbs is a writer for the Guardian, Independent and Time Out.

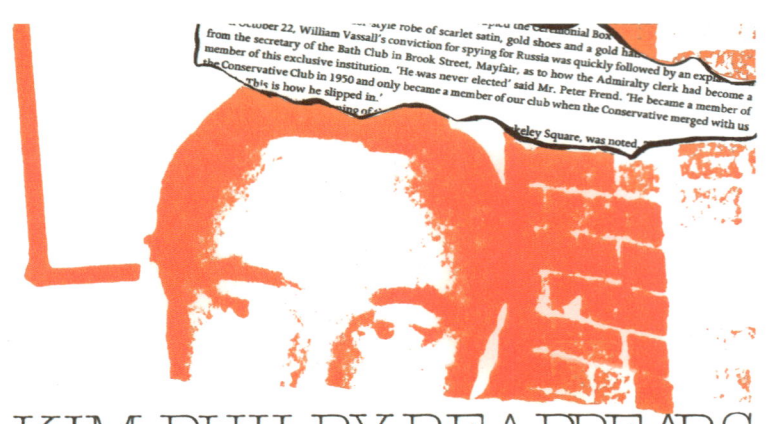

KIM·PHILBY·REAPPEARS
JOY DIVISION - A CERT
AIN RATIO - SECTION 25
NEW OSBOURNE — FEB 7
FAC FOR CITY FUNDS !

(£1¼)

A CERTAIN RATIO
DVRVTTI COLVMN
BLVRT - AUG 21
RAFTERS OXFORD RD
£1·50n

OHNE TITEL PRESENTS

Left Top
*Poster for Joy Division,
Jon Savage 1980.*

Left Bottom
*Poster for A Certain Ration,
Jon Savage 1980.*

Right
*Poster for The Electric Circus,
Courtesy Jon Savage.*

THE ELECTRIC CIRCUS

Collyhurst St. Off Rochdale Rd. Manchester
Manchester's Latest & Greatest Live Rock Venue
Tel: 061-205 9411
1 MILE FROM CITY CENTRE

**EVERY FRIDAY — PROGRESSIVE ROCK
EVERY SATURDAY AND SUNDAY — NEW WAVE**

FRIDAY SEPT. 2nd	**RADIO STARS**
SATURDAY SEPT. 3rd	**SLAUGHTER and the DOGS** plus THE DRONES
	THE DRONES plus SLAUGHTER and the DOGS
SUNDAY SEPT. 4th	**THE BOYS**
FRIDAY SEPT. 9th	**STRIFE**
SATURDAY SEPT. 10th	**SUBURBAN STUDS** plus SNATCH
SUNDAY SEPT. 11th	**THE MODELS** plus STILETTO
THURSDAY SEPT. 15th	**US -** SOUND SPECTACULAR ROCK COMPETITION
FRIDAY SEPT. 16th	**THE PIRATES** (Out of their Skulls Tour)
SATURDAY SEPT. 17th	**ULTRAVOX**
SUNDAY SEPT. 18th	**THE MOTORS** plus SCREW DRIVER
FRIDAY SEPT. 23rd	**KILLER**
SATURDAY SEPT. 24th	**THE REZILLOS**
SUNDAY SEPT. 25th	**THE SLITS**
FRIDAY SEPT. 30th	**JENNY HANNS LION**
SAT. & SUN. OCT. 1st, 2nd	**NEW WAVE —** Benefit Gig for PAT SEEDS SCANNER APPEAL FUND Bands to be announced

Please note from time to time the dates of Bands may change. For latest details please see Friday's Evening News or listen to Piccadilly Radios 'What's On' Guide between one and two every Friday.
Tickets available from Virgin Records and Electric Circus Box Office

LATE BAR TILL 2 a.m. — STUDENT DISCOUNT

P.T.O.

16 – Unknown Pleasure: The Haçienda

Unknown Pleasure: The Haçienda

Jon Savage

Jon Savage reports on how the Haçienda nightclub arose from the cultural wastelands levelled by punk rock and James' Anderton's police force, and how the importance of the club's forgotten early 'arts lab' days before the arrival of the 24-hour Party People should not be overlooked in assessing its influence.

Jon Savage by Linder Sterling, Whalley Range (1978).

I walked through the city limits
Someone talked me in to do it
Attracted by some force within it
Had to close my eyes to get close to it
Ian Curtis for Joy Division: 'Interzone' (1978)

The relation of music to physical place is as ill-documented as it is central. Music is a social force — even when it is being anti-social — that works in tandem with environment, place and time to create sound that has the requisite physiological effect. The more that it harmonises with these factors, the greater impact it has.

Who can now think of the early Beatles without mentally replaying the summer 1962 Granada footage of 'Some Other Guy': crunching R&B + tiny physical space = raw power? Is there any greater testament to the corrosive effect of their global fame than the films of them playing in huge, disconnected stadia, their out-of-tune renderings obliterated by thousands of avian shrieks?

Such questions became particularly relevant during the late 1970's because of the intimate relationship between punk and a new kind of urbanism. Through a combination of factors — a deep recession, failed slum clearance, flight to the suburbs — many major urban centres in the US and the UK were near derelict: industrial wastelands out of William Burroughs or JG Ballard.

These were the kind of areas that Frederic Thrasher, in his seminal sociological work on Chicago gangs (*The Gang*, 1926), had called twilight zones, 'regions of conflict' that acted 'like a frontier'. As he exhaustively researched, these voids offered up a window into another kind of urban life that would be filled by the young, the heedless and the reckless.

Whether in New York or London, Cleveland or Manchester, there are many accounts by the participants in what would become called punk rock as to the possibilities opened up by these 'Blank spaces and empty places'.[1] Punk magazine contributor Mary Harron saw near-bankrupt New York as 'almost mystically wonderful', while Joe Strummer was actively involved in the large squatting community that settled around Elgin Avenue, London W9, in 1975.

London punk was saturated in images of a decaying city in conflict — tower-blocks and urban riot, blank stares and brick walls — that matched the location of key venues in forgotten districts: most significantly, the Roxy, in derelict Covent Garden. In this tiny, scuzzy basement an intimate relation of audience/performer could be perfected: heckling + feedback/overload > attraction + repulsion.

However, this claustrophobia became hard to live with. As London punk moved into larger venues, it took with it the Capital's habitual bad temper. When the The Clash played the Rainbow in May 1977, the chaos that they habitually summoned up in small spaces erupted in a spontaneous deconstruction of the venue. (This also occurred in the Manchester Apollo six months later, but it felt more joyous.)

I moved to Manchester in April 1979, and was immediately struck by the large swathes of dereliction, particularly in the ring around the city centre where new experiments in modern living had produced only the concrete rebus of Hulme. This was a new, occluded environment, ruled by a hostile, moralistic police chief whose force regarded it as their job to rule your everyday life.

As it happened, the key to getting around the city was right under my nose. I'd already been in touch with Tony Wilson and Rob Gretton, and as soon I arrived I was involved with their group, Joy Division. I saw them at the Factory, went to Strawberry Studios where Martin Hannett was producing Unknown Pleasures, talked tactics with Rob in his Chorlton flat.

Quite apart from Ian Curtis' hypnotic, unfiltered stage performances, the music of Joy Division perfectly fitted their adopted city. As Liz Naylor later stated, they were a true 'ambient band': they totally reflected their environment. Not just in the lyric and title of 'Interzone', but their Janus-faced sound: brutal and performance-art con frontational live, psychedelic and dreamy on record.

To the centre of the city where all roads meet, waiting for you
To the depths of the ocean where all hopes sank, searching for you Ian Curtis for Joy Division, 'Shadowplay' (1978)

Much more so than London — where there still were vestiges of prosperity — Manchester punk was truly the product of isolation and dereliction. It seemed as though all decent humans had left the inner city and its immediate outer ring as soon as the sun had gone down, leaving what Naylor proudly called 'the scum of the earth': the poor, the prostituted, the punks and the hard-core dissident.

Some of these outcasts populated clubs like the Electric Circus (in the midst of destroyed 1930's blocks in Collyhurst), the Ranch (a rent-boy bar attached to Foo Foo's Palace, in Dale Street, central Manchester) or, from 1978 on, the PSV/Russell Club or the edge of Hulme. These were the laboratories for a music and a culture that would finally throw off the domination of the Capital to create 21st Century Manchester.

In tandem with their super-intense live shows, Joy Division were very futuristic: their use of new synthesiser technology, their utilitarian clothing, the deep, almost mystical relation with their environment. During the summer of 1979, they helped me to map my new home, with its rows of sleeping suburban semis, and curious, claustrophobic comforts broken up by sudden spasms of violence.

Unknown Pleasures became the soundtrack to a series of nocturnal, psychogeographical wanderings through Miles Platting, Gorton, Harpurhey, Trafford Park. This was Manchester's industrial detritus, peopled by the ghosts of the countless unknown who had built the 19th Century futuropolis and the 20th Century manufacturing powerhouse.

Despite the white-light intensity of their performances, there was a very dark side to Joy Division — as indeed there was to Manchester at that time: a Lovecraftian sense of crawling, impending doom. This was added to a Kafka-esque sense of being a pawn in someone else's game — an all-pervasive sense of paranoia amply assisted by the exquisite attentions of Chief Constable James Anderton's armies.[2] The small scene that developed around Joy Division and Factory — which was only one of a number of city scenes — offered a community of disparate but driven souls. Whether by accident or design, Tony Wilson and Rob Gretton sought to bring a number of very disparate people together: because they would help, because they were interesting, because they hustled, just because.

The result was akin to a contemporary version of the Warhol Factory, albeit on a much smaller, localised scale, as the poor and desperate, the young with nothing to lose, rubbed shoulders with gay people, intellectuals, urban professionals. Roles were fluid, and the possibilities were there to be taken: Wilson was a great spotter and catalyst, if you wanted to do something, he would help.

17 — Unknown Pleasure: The Haçienda

This community was severely bruised, but not broken by Ian Curtis' suicide in May 1980. After due pause, the three remaining musicians regrouped as New Order. By 1981, they were moving out of the numb phase recorded on *Movement* and making dance records like 'Everything's Gone Green' which, with its Moroder pulse and war whoops, sounded like spring after a long winter.

Factory were still releasing records that matched great music with Peter Saville's brilliant designs: OMD's 'Electricity', with its Braille, black-on-black cover and, in particular, the collaboration with Ben Kelly for the Section 25 'Girls Don't Count' 45 which, with its geometrics and attention to (tracing paper) texture, now seems like a dry-run for the greater project a year or so later.

This was an itinerant time for the former Russell Club regulars: the search for a new home was on. Despite the media attention focussed on the Factory scene, it was small and unwelcome in mainstream dance Meccas. The PSV was no longer available. An attempt at opening up the derelict deco New Osborne on Oldham Road as the new Factory had proved unsuccessful.

Apart from occasional one-offs like the New Order show at the Ritz, the main focus in 1980 and 1981 was the Beach Club, run by a collective that included Richard Boon and Susanne O'Hara out of an obscure Lesbian bar called Oozits, in Shudehill. On its two floors you could see films like Peter Watkins' banned *The War Game* or, in late July 1980, New Order's first tentative show.

Ignored by the London media, the experimental, almost Arts Lab feel of the Beach Club marked the transition between what had been and what was to come. Simple rock shows in tatty clubs were not enough. There was the desire for something more ambitious that would place a marker for the future, still dimly recognised, of Manchester as 21st Century culture city.

Frustration with the existing venues was a part of it, but the Factory roster of the time speaks of more than just a rock label: there were droning post-punkers, psychedelic experimenters, poets, folk singers and confrontational, post-situ bands like the Royal Family And The Poor – whose 1982 12" single, 'Art on 45', is a forgotten classic from this period.

1981 was the moment of Eighties modernism: the time when avant-garde white rock and electronica and avant-garde, street-level blackamerican culture began to come together. It was the moment when a few people in Manchester suddenly had more in common with New York than anyone in their home-town. Punk had razed the territory: now was the time for reconstruction.

> "It was just an attitude. It has an original, unique and regional quality to it. It was like-minded people from different disciplines homing in on a common cause." Ben Kelly, interviewed by Jon Savage, 1992

The idea came from Rob Gretton. "I wanted a club where I could ogle women," he told me, with typical self-deprecating earthiness, in 1992. But the real impetus came from the buzz of the PSV/ Russell nights filtered through the new Manhattan nightclubs — 'groovy spaces' like Danceteria and Hurrah's, which acted both as venues and dischotheques.

Although all concerned would have disavowed it, there was an altruistic motive behind the new club. "Tony, Rob, Alan (Erasmus) were totally into the idea of putting some of the money they'd made back into Manchester," the Haçienda's first manager, Howard 'Ginger' Jones told me in 1992. "The whole Factory tenet was more than just musical, it was to effect people's environment."

The site was found: a former pleasure boat salesroom near the west end of Whitworth Street, parallel to the railway viaduct. This cavernous space backed onto the canal and was at one end of what would become the strip between Whitworth Street (The Cornerhouse, The Ritz, the future post-Anderton 'gay village') and Knott Mill/Deansgate (TJ Davidson's, the Boardwalk).

Despite considerable obstruction from the police and a massive budget overspend (up to seventy-five percent), the club opened in May 1982. Designed by Ben Kelly and Peter Saville, it was not post-modern but hyper-modern space — informed by that early 80's cultural moment of optimism and forward motion. It was called the Haçienda and given a Factory number: Fac 51.

The name had come from the manifesto by Ivan Chtcheglov, who in 1953 had sought to give shape to the nocturnal wanderings undertaken by him and the other downbeat regulars of Chez Moineau. Acknowledging the ghosts of the past, he called for a new urbanism that re-zoned the city in terms of the imagination, in terms of a constant, perpetual change in perspective.

'You'll never see the haçienda,' Chtcheglov wrote. 'It doesn't exist. The haçienda must be built.' And so the nightclub arose in this spirit of paradox and perverse auto-critique: both Wilson and Gretton were familiar with pro-situ urbanism and its rhetoric, thanks to the readily available translation by Christopher Gray, *Leaving the 20th Century*.[3]

As well as representing an ambitious attempt to re-zone a forgotten corner of the city, the Haçienda broke with convention in several ways. It was not reliant on the existing club culture of the day — the cattle-market of Rotters, bare-bones rock venues like Rafters — nor did it simply have one function: it could be venue or disco, members' club or arts lab, with spoken-word events or film shows.

The interior was heavily and beautifully designed, in startling and primary colours — yellow and silver — with imaginative development of industrial textures and themes. The geometrical straight lines of the décor and the fittings were carried on through into the graphics for the club: the membership cards, the gig posters, the Gay Traitor Bar cocktail list.

After the decaying grunge of most Manchester venues, the Haçienda was a real shock: in the early days, it was as though the future had beamed in, and you were in on the secret. In a still poor and dangerous inner city, the club was a safe space: a haven where women, gay people, black and white, the weird and the dissident could gather without any threat or hassle.

Entering from the then deserted street, you'd pass into the space beyond, which would be booming with the electro of the day. First there was the dining area, with the stairs down to the Gay Traitor Bar on the left, and the proscenium arch on the right leading to the dancefloor, bar, seating booths and the stage — situated off to one side rather than directly in the eyeline, along the end wall.

This was the most controversial aspect of the design. The strange placing of the stage area made the regular weekly gigs a real scrum, as hundreds pressed into an enclosed area to see a wide range of acts: the Birthday Party, the Sisters of Mercy, Orange Juice, Blancmange, A Certain Ratio, Einstürzende Neubauten, Grandmaster Flash, the Cramps, the Smiths, Madonna... and New Order themselves.

Above the stage there were two large video monitors, which would show either Ikon recorded material or VJ Claude Bessy's patented mix of porn, splatter and found images. To stage right was the enclosed DJ booth, home to the likes of Hewan Clarke, Mike Pickering and, for a few months in 1982, myself. Neither this position nor the sound was ideal, but it kept away the requests for Killing Joke.

The club wasn't as empty as legend has it. At the time it didn't seem like a disaster, more like an open space for new opportunities. People didn't have to dance: they could meet and talk, get their hair cut (by Andrew Berry at Swing), plan magazines, groups, fashion events and videos. The club was home to a late 1982 Granada Television shoot for *Patient*, by Ludus.

In October 1982, the crowds packed in for *The Final Academy*, the event featuring William Burroughs and others, and sat down on the dance floor. Sitting on the dance floor? Fantastic! This would be a total breach of etiquette in today's rigidly programmed club culture, but now seems like an index of why the early Haçienda was so interesting — and why it has been written out of history.

The onset of E culture from 1986 on and, during 1989, the Madchester media hype, was based on a euphoric reality. However it has dominated the framing of Factory and the Haçienda ever since — most notably in Michael Winterbottom's *24 Hour Party People* — to the exclusion of the more fluid definition of urban and cultural space that the label and the club first offered.

As if it wasn't enough justification in itself, the club's early Arts Lab ambience laid the foundations for what would occur half a decade later. Seen in this light, the Haçienda is an inspiration: not just because it was there that people took drugs or danced all night, but because it represented an imaginative, futuristic and practical attempt to redraw the city's map for its youth.

Jon Savage is an award-winning writer, broadcaster and music journalist. His book, *Teenage: The Creation of Youth Culture*, a history of the concept of 'teenager', was published in 2007.

[1] *Pere Ubu, My Dark Ages (1976). David Thomas on the new urbanism: 'the city I loved was one that everyone else hated, it was totally deserted, people fled when the sun went down. It was run down, but we thought it was beautiful at the time of youth when you're prone to romanticism. I wondered at what point a civilisation hits its peak and begins to decline: all those deserted cities, the jungle overgrows them, at what point does the city die? At what point do the people who live there no longer understand the vision of the builders? A city should clearly reflect the vision of the builders. All those factors were why we loved Cleveland at that point, we felt that we owned it, because nobody else wanted it. "A lot of the people in the band (Pere Ubu) were involved in that urban Pioneer thing that was going on in America in the 70s, when people moved back to the inner cities. That was what the Plaza was, it was a really nice old building in a terrible neighbourhood. It wasn't because we liked darkness, a lot of us were involved in that, loved the city, appreciated the almost naive vision of the people who had built it.'*

[2] *Note the appearance of Anderton as a sinister figure in Malcolm Whitehead's contemporary film, Joy Division (1979).*

[3] *In spring / summer 1982, as the nightclub was being launched, I made a programme for Granada TV local programmes with Wilson about the history of Trafford Park which featured him quoting heavily from the large format green paperback on camera.*

18 — Unknown Pleasure: The Haçienda

The Flash Artists

8 key artists for Corridor8

These pages will form an important annual feature of Corridor8, providing a changing platform for artists to display their work, make ideological and artistic statements, provide biographical details and voice assessments of what is happening that is exciting in contemporary art. At present, many artists in the region exhibit and conduct their main business in London, Paris or New York. As witnessed by the article within these pages on Paul Bradley, it is possible, given the will and desire to successfully invest, to make this region as attractive a proposition for the sighting and buying of art as any pre-existing centres of art and business.

With many established artists from outside the region having shown at venues along the SuperCity corridor, it is about time to brag a little about the exemplary quality of work being generated from within that same stretch. By refocusing attention towards the corridor, let's see if we can challenge investors in art to look again at the rich and diverse material on offer here, and see the possibilities inherent in setting up stall in the region. Let's see if we can encourage gallerists and buyers, commissioners and entrepreneurs to create a going concern, and put a stop to an ongoing one. Here are just some of the people who prove that they need look no further.

We begin with Dublin-based Isabel Nolan who perfectly marries an intuitive intellect with a disciplined hand, creating a unique and eclectic body of work. In her search for meaning she utilises needlework, abstract geometry, painting and found objects to uncover the hidden energy in things. In this universe of competing forces each element is able to hold its own and make its presence felt. It is art by any means necessary, with a signature that is constantly changing.

Based in Hull, Bob Levene is an artist who embraces the inconclusive, ongoing and unpredictable. Her work resounds with a poetic sensibility that defies categorisation, but with a focus on the nature of perception and sound. Adopting pseudo-scientific strategies and anthropological methods of recording to analyse the 'nature' of things, she investigates time, distance and communication. In her efforts, with limited resources and limited tools, she uncovers with wit and a guile-free sincerity a finely balanced poetics of perception that takes us beyond the 'truth' of things and into the realm of the absurd.

In Manchester, Rachael Goodyear's subtly enigmatic and disturbing dream-like vignettes single-handedly re-established drawing as a serious activity within the city's art scene. Her authoritative yet consistently fragile pencil and paint works already have a huge fanbase outside of the city, and she is leading the way in an area of practice that many 'serious' art world people had seen little value in until she came along.

Hailing from Sheffield, Simon Le Ruez's subversive humour and disturbed metaphorical landscapes and sculptures intimates a resonating darkness that belies the calmness on the surface of things. His intimate constructions and titles suggest sexual tensions buried in the everyday moment, filtered through the wistful reminiscences of a carewom melancholic disposition. With a kind of perverted Romantic expression, objects are endowed with a dark matter whose vibrating fields scupper their benign appearance.

Freee Collective in Sheffield bring together the combined talents of Dave Beech, Andy Hewitt and Mel Jordan. With a shared interest in the critiquing of everyday experience, they formulate agit-prop texts and events whose didactic sloganeering seeks to counter-balance the weight of persuasive advertising and information that surrounds us. With an emphasis on the authority of text they are a team on a mission to drive a spike into the language of control.

Matthew Houlding is resident in Todmorden, Yorkshire but represented by Galleries in both Liverpool and Dresden. His escapist architectural models, lovingly constructed from the detritus of everyday materials, are imbued with an insistent modernist longing tempered by the reality and physical limitations of the material world. Like the daydream of a perfect future from which you will wake up and have to put out the recycling bins, he transforms the everyday into a fragile visionary landscape that the viewer is invited to return to again and again in the search for a lost horizon.

Rory MacBeth from Leeds is single-minded in his pursuit of an idea. Widely shown in the UK and Italy he has forged a reputation for himself with his idiosyncratic take on gallery tours and art fairs, overturning expectations by presenting estate agents and creating a smokescreen of false information to the public on gallery tours at the Tate. This askance take on predictability is both entertaining and revealing, especially when it bleeds out in the urban landscape in the fresh lick of paint he gives to burnt-out vehicles or the leaves on trees he replaces with cut-outs for the winter months.

In Liverpool we have Paul Rooney, a writer and video maker who's work is rooted in other people's stories. Working with themes of public life and work, he personalises the impersonal tasks of gallery staff, night workers and call centre staff, tour guides and plastic packaging designers and brings them to a kind of ecstatic life through comedy, theatre, song and the act of filmmaking itself.

Isabel Nolan

Dublin

Nolan in her studio.

Top Left
Crushing Spring (2007). 250 x 200cm. Cotton, linen, embroidery silk and thread. Courtesy Kerlin Gallery, Dublin.

Right
Jesus, you look so sad (2007). 50 x 60cm. Watercolour and paper on canvas. Courtesy Kerlin Gallery, Dublin.

Isabel Nolan's work is both sceptical of and empathetic to our relentless compulsion to understand everything – from our inner lives to the inscrutable nature of the universe. Recurring themes are the intimacies and distances inherent in relationships; belief, desire, loneliness, self-consciousness, and the ambiguity of language. Sources for forms of the work include literature; the natural world, and depictions of it; and, also, abstract imagery.

Nolan's practice encompasses drawings, paintings, animation, mixed media and fibreglass sculptures and, most recently, embroidery and fabric wall-hangings. The work exudes a quiet confidence and clearly attests to the pleasure she takes in using a variety of materials, in drawing and making objects.

Though there are frequent shifts in tone, between coldness, bemusement, melancholia and yearning, a point of entry common to much of Nolan's work is its recognition of our seemingly implacable need to define our situation and our relationships with others. The work both acknowledges and reprises the role of subjectivity, and the ways in which language, aspirations, and the want of knowledge, affect understanding and the designation of meaning.

The work is conceived as a means of acting – of making a new thing – in the form of images, texts and objects that have no overt message but whose very raison d'être is to assert the value of, and complexity, involved in response and description.

Text courtesy Kerlin Gallery

20 – Isabel Nolan

Biog

Isabel Nolan was born in 1974 and lives in Dublin. Her first one-person exhibition was at the Proposition Gallery, Belfast, in 1998, and since then she has had solo exhibitions at the Goethe Institute (2003), Project Arts Centre (2005), Temple Bar Gallery & Studios (2005) and Four (2005), in Dublin, and in The Studio, Glasgow, as part of *Glasgow International 2006*. She represented *Ireland at the 2005 Venice Biennale* in a group exhibition, Ireland at Venice 2005, which was subsequently presented at the Lewis Glucksman Gallery, Cork, in 2006. In 2006 she also produced an off-site project *Together is Enough* for the Douglas Hyde Gallery, Dublin. She has participated in numerous group exhibitions including *How Things Turn Out* (2002) and *Tír na nÓg* (2004), both at The Irish Museum of Modern Art, Dublin, *Superbia 1 & 2*, Cork (2003 & 2005), *The Yugoslav Biennial for Young Artists*, Serbia-Montenegro (2004), Coalesce — With All Due Intent, Model Art & Niland Gallery, Sligo (2004), *Views from an Island* (Collection of IMMA), Millenium Monument, Beijing and Shanghai Art Museum, China, Mediation Biennale, Poznan (2008) and Micro-narratives, Musée d'art moderne de Saint Etienne (2008).

Nolan had her first solo exhibition at the Kerlin Gallery in early 2007 and presented new work at both the Douglas Hyde gallery, Dublin and ARTSPACE, New Zealand in 2008. Nolan is currently part of *Coalesce : Happenstance*, SMART, Amsterdam. Her work is represented in the collection of the Irish Museum of Modern Art, City Gallery the Hugh Lane, Dublin and in various collections, public and private, in Ireland and abroad.

Kerlin Gallery Eimear O'Raw
t. + 3531 670 9093 e. eimear@kerlin.ie

Q&A

What are you working on currently?
Small scale sculptures and paintings. I'll be doing a solo show in the Kerlin Gallery at the end of 2009, so I'm thinking about what I want to do for that.

Where did you study?
In Dublin at the National College of Art and Design for my BA and I did a stint of reading/research in University College of Dublin as an MLitt student. Later I did an MA in Visual Culture at the Dun Laoghaire Institute of Design and Technology.

Who influenced your early years as an artist or art student?
As a student I'd say Kurt Vonnegut.

Have you ever seen, read about or heard of an artwork or art activity (other than your own) that made you think art could be significant?
Yes... it's a vague question. Significant in what sense?

Do you work on several things at once?
Sort of, I start things and often leave them a long time before I do more to them, so there are always things ongoing but my brain doesn't do multi-tasking very well so I tend to focus on one thing at a time.

Do you enjoy making art?
In the narrow sense, yes — I like actually making objects, crafting things with my hands. In regard to the broader sense of making artworks I'm quite ambivalent, there are good and bad times, hills and valleys.

How do you deal with titles in your work?
I generally think about them a lot — sometimes they are absolutely crucial to the work. Often enough I'll have a title straightaway, but now and again I don't and I'll run out of time and have to decide really quickly, and I find that frustrating.

What is it like to live and work in Dublin?
Well, there are some really interesting and talented people here, but there aren't a lot of public and commercial spaces, so there is a limited amount of shows to see (and hence, opportunities) — but I still don't manage to see them all. In any case, it's well connected for travelling elsewhere to see shows and people, also Dublin seems to be edging on to the radar of travelling international curators, et cetera. Economically it's tough, as it's an expensive city, and that was before the recession hit. However, there are tax breaks for artists, which is terrific. Radio is pretty awful here, though, and the people I vote for are never in government.

Why do you stay here?
Habit — friends/family/dog. Dublin has its moments. Also I live near the sea and within walking distance of the city, that's a nice situation.

Who or what has made the biggest contribution to the contemporary art scene in the Dublin region?
I'd need to list all the big, public and commercial spaces and a dozen individuals. It's a small enough place, so anyone who is enthusiastic and gets things going can make a big difference. Cliver Dowling had a really important gallery back in the day, 70's and early 80's I think, and he went on to advise at the Arts Council, which adds up to decades of contribution. Also Aer Lingus (years ago they used to sponsor flights for artists), and budget air travel in general.

Who else should we be watching?
Bea McMahon, Walker and Walker, Garrett Phelan, Mark Garry, Ronan McCrea, Dennis McNulty, Sarah Pierce and Alan Phelan — all artists. Curators and writers — Vaari Claffey, Georgina Jackson, Sarah Glennie, Declan Long and Pádraic E Moore. And all of them are physically very attractive people, so they are especially nice to watch.

What curators and galleries do you admire, and why (locally or internationally)?
Locally — Vaari Claffey. She's worked with nearly everyone of a certain generation and has a really dedicated and rigorous art-brain. Currently she has a space called Gallery For One and she publishes a fanzine called Feint. Lee Welch's gallery, Four, has consistently had really interesting shows in the three years its been going. Sarah Glennie, who is with the Irish Film Institute now. Commonplace Amateur Projects, run by Sally Timmons, is another very interesting venture.

What are your plans for the future? If you had unlimited funds, what artwork would you make?
Those are too hard to answer, plus I can't give away my plans for the ultimate artwork. If I had lots of cash I'd hire an architect (Aoife Donnelly, based in London), build a house, an amazing studio, and I'd hire someone to fill in forms and to talk on the phone on my behalf — I hate the phone.

If you could own any work of art, what would it be?
I don't know — I wish I had a perfect answer for this, of all the questions. I can't choose one or even two things — I'd prefer a private jet, time and the cash to plant hectares of trees so I could visit various works.

If you weren't an artist what job would you like/rather be doing?
I really don't know. I like the idea of being the person who writes indexes for books. A good index is a wondrous and useful entity.

Do you have any advice for this year's graduates?
Sorry, but not really. Have they any for me? How about, keep making more/new/better work...

Below Left
Disorder is always increasing (2008). 108 x 42 x 42cm. Wood, jesmonite, paint. Courtesy Kerlin Gallery, Dublin.

Below Right
Jesus, you look so tired (2007). 40 x 50cm. Watercolour and paper on canvas. Courtesy Kerlin Gallery, Dublin.

21 — Isabel Nolan

Bob Levene

Hull

Levene in the Finnish Archipelago.

Top
Handmade (2002 & 2007). Performance / Record / Installation.

Right
Metal shoes from Action, Delay, Sound [working title] (2008). Performance.

Using recorded sound and video, performance and wider communication methods, such as cartography, Bob Levene questions our understanding of distance, speed and time and the contradictions and conflicts that arise when trying to represent our perceived world through another medium.

In recent years her work has drawn from the landscape where she explores how our understanding of the world is shaped by the limitations of the body we inhabit. Working with tools that measure, objectify and give our world order alongside the subjective experience, the work touches on the psychology of perception. Representation and the notion of truth are at the core of her practice.

Text courtesy of the artist

Biog

Bob Levene has performed at The London Musicians' Collective 16th Annual Experimental Music Festival, Slovenia's International Computer Arts Festival and will be part of BBC Radio 3 and Sonic Arts Networks 2009 Cut & Splice Festival. She has been artist in residence at The Yorkshire Sculpture Park and was commissioned to produce new work for a solo show at Cornerhouse, Manchester.

Other exhibitions have included Globe Gallery, North Shields; FA Projects, London; Peterborough Digital Arts, *Captured* at the National Review of Live Art and *Future 50* at Project Space Leeds Gallery, at Leeds. Awards include an Arts Council International Fellowship in Colima, Mexico and an Artsadmin Mid-Career Bursary. She recently returned from a residency in Turku in Finland where she was filming in the Islands of the Archipelago.

She also collaborates with artist, musician and lecturer Rob Gawthrop under the name Automated Noise Ensemble.

w. *www.automatednoiseensemble.co.uk*

Q&A

What are you working on currently?

I've been thinking about time in relation to distance, speed and memory, how fast something appears to be going depending on its proximity to you, and how fast you are moving in relation to it.

During my first weekend in Finland, I went south to the Archipelago. I took a ferry ride to the furthest inhabited island called Utö, with a population of twenty. From the city of Turku it took one and a half hours by coach and a further five hours by ferry. It was isolated and beautifully bleak... For the last four weeks I've been going back to the Archipelago, filming one particular ferry route between Pargas and Nauvo. It's only a one-mile journey and takes just over eight minutes. Pointing my camera away from the ferry I have been focusing on the horizon line and the islands that pass by. It has a range of different speeds, the speed of the sea, the sky and the islands, which all vary depending on distance from the camera and of course the speed of the ferry. As the light fades so does the sense of speed and distance. I'm hoping it will be become a film piece, but it's too early to say.

I am also continuing with my interest in maps, measurements and the imagination in a series that brings together ideas of recorded time, speed, data graphs and the journey. Before I came to Finland I was living in Brooklyn, New York for three months. I visited The American Museum of Natural History and was overwhelmed by the amount of tourists with digital cameras and how often they would take a photo. For some, their whole time was viewed through the screen of their camera. It was as if the only memory they will have when looking back at that photograph is the memory of taking the photograph. This relentless happy snapping got me thinking about recording time, taking moments from time and the contrast between our experience of 'real time' as a continuous stream and our different approaches to measuring, documenting and recording it. I wanted to document my 'New York Time' without being too bogged down with selections and choices, so I chose to mark onto a map where I had been that day, the ground I had covered.

Where did you study?

After dropping out of my A-Levels in 1993 I was gently pushed by some kind teachers and friends (to whom I am eternally grateful) onto a BTEC National Diploma at Epsom School of Art and Design. I continued straight on to do a BA in Fine Art at Hull School of Art and Design, University of Lincoln and Humberside, and just over two years later in 2001 I completed an Msc in Electronic Imaging at Duncan of Jordanstone College of Art and Design, University of Dundee.

Who influenced your early years as an art student?

As a student I was always hungry to see new work. When I went back to London to visit my parents I'd always go into town and see as many shows as I could. It didn't matter what it was, I'd go and see it. I was lucky to have a lot of really good tutors during all my courses, Hull in particular. Clare Charnley and Helmut Lemke played a big part in the direction I took, but it was with Rob Gawthrop that the debating continued well past my degree until it became a collaborative practice under the name of Automated Noise Ensemble, which is still going eight years on.

It was also Rob who curated regular experimental film screenings that included the likes of Dziga Vertov, Len Lye, GPO Films, Stan Brakhage, Bruce Conner, Michael Snow, John Smith — the list goes on — that had a great impact on my work. At the time I was also looking at the performance camera relationship in the work of Bruce Nauman and Vito Acconci.

But if I had to choose just a few it would probably be the work of Alvin Lucier, particularly *I am sitting in a room*, 1969. It opened up the subject of listening, and how we listen differently to speech, sound, music and noise. He works with the physicality of sound and acoustical phenomena but also makes it personal by using his own voice and highlighting his stutter. The most interesting thing about this piece is how the speech turns into sound and the sound turns into music but its impossible to tell at what point this actually happens. Then there was Anthony McCall's *Line Describing A Cone*; conceptually whole this piece is amazing to experience. It brings together the sculptural elements of film, time and light and provokes wonderment with something so simple. It has elegance and beauty whilst maintaining a structural rigor. I just wished I could have seen it when smoking was still allowed in cinemas. I was also into the work of Christian Marclay, particularly *Footsteps*, 1989, *Record without a Cover*, 1985 and *Guitar Drag*, 2000. I liked his treatment and playfulness with recorded music and instruments and how he works with the physicality of the music object and its image.

Do you work on several things at once?

Yes, but they tend to all be related to one particular area of interest. Take the work I did earlier in the year whilst I was in residence at Yorkshire Sculpture Park. I'd already done some research into early forms of long-distance communications and knew I wanted to utilise the full size of the park, to explore ideas around human scale and an individual's perception of distance. What I ended up with was five new works, some of which are still in progress. In *As Far As The Eye Can See* I worked with a surveyor from Ordnance Survey to produce five cut-out OS maps that plotted the furthest horizon line I could see at a 360-degree turn.

The bringing together of a scientific reading of the topography of the land and my experience within it was also explored in *Measured Sound*, a performance still in progress. I divided the field with flags into three sections of 340 metres (the distance which sound travels in a second). Whistles and trumpets were played at each flag whilst being transmitted via walkie-talkies. This was listened to from the first flag (0 Seconds), creating a delay between the acoustic sound (speed of sound) and transmitted sounds (speed of light). Of course the further away the whistles and trumpets got, the longer the delay became, and the harder the acoustic sound was to hear. By the final flag (just under 1 km) it was almost inaudible.

The contrast between the speed of light and sound, the thunder-and-lightning effect, was pushed further with the piece *Sound, Action, Delay (Working Title)*, a performance where I stand on a metal box placed on the top of a bank or hill. Wearing specially built metal shoes, I jump up and down on a metal box. The audience stands at least 340 metres away, so the sound takes over a second to arrive, making the sound out of sync with the image of me jumping.

Do you enjoy making art?

One of the things I like about being an artist is the places it takes you. I don't just mean geographically, but more the odd things you find yourself doing. Like the other day when the crew of the ferry I'd been filming on invited me into the control room to have some tea to warm up, or debating with a surveyor from Ordnance Survey about what field we were looking at. Making art gives me permission to be curious, question, experiment and play for a living. I can't think of anything better. It's a constant challenge intellectually, technically and financially. I also like working for myself, although it's not a job.

How do you deal with titles in your work?

Badly, I hate figuring out titles for my work, I'm crap at it. It's not made any easier by the fact that it comes so easily in my collaborative practice with Rob Gawthrop. It seems so straightforward and descriptive when I'm working with Automative Noise Ensemble (ANE), for instance *Cymbals*, an installation that shows two cymbals and turntable strings for the performance that involves sticking bits of string onto turntables. Such titling makes sense for the type of work ANE makes. My own work doesn't always suit that; *As Far As The Eye Can See* and *Hand Drawn Map Collection* are the only exceptions.

Where do you live / work?

At the time of writing I'm on a series of travels and residencies, and living and working in Turku, Finland, prior to which I was in New York for three months. But for the most part of the last ten or so years I've been living in Hull.

What is it like to live and work here?

Everyone has their own view of Hull. When I arrived there I found it was a vibrant place that was under the radar, and that attracted a good bunch of misfits who would do stuff off their own backs. They seemed concerned about what art is and what it can do... Hull Time Based Arts was a big part of the Hull art world that I frequented, from being a volunteer... There was a time later on when it became a frustrating place to live. It is a small city, with a relatively small art scene, so when the art school was closed down it had a big impact. With no new art students, researchers or visiting lecturers coming in and a lot of people leaving, it felt like Hull had received a major blow. Although this period did trigger the formation of Hull Art Lab, which I ran alongside Rob Gawthrop and Espen Jensen, and Resound Community Partnerships with Jo Millett, Rick Welton and Audrey Okyere Fosu, both of which were a steep learning curve and extremely rewarding, if a little exhausting. In recent times Hull seems to have a greater ambition with a new art school and the likes of Espen and others who continue to work tirelessly away at making things happen. I'm glad I went to study there and remained for so long; it gave a good grounding.

What curators and galleries do you admire, and why?

There is a lot of interesting stuff going on, too much to mention. In the last year or so I've been lucky enough to work with Ben Drew and the London Musicians Collective, and curator William Rose who formerly co-ran the Evolution Experimental Film festival in Leeds and now works with no.w.here lab in London. I'm keen on organisations and curators who are willing to take risks and put faith in the artist to try something new, and who have a passion and care for what they do. I'm also interested in the bringing together of historical and contemporary work, and the broad definitions of experimental film, sound and music, which the Kill Your Timid Notion festival, in Dundee, does so well with its open and genuinely friendly atmosphere. There are also a number of organisations that I haven't visited but have admired from afar, like Grizedale Arts in Cumbria, and The Star and Shadow cinema in Newcastle, and The Center For Land Use Interpretation in Los Angeles, an organisation that engages in research, classification, extrapolation and exhibition of issues around land and landscape.

Rachel Goodyear

Manchester / Salford

Goodyear at home.

Rachel Goodyear's drawings present captured moments where characters reside within an existence where social etiquette no longer, or maybe never applied.

She looks for unlikely relationships in everything she encounters. From this constant everyday cross-referencing she creates carefully constructed coincidences that are delicate in their nature and unsettling in their content.

Text courtesy of the artist

Biog

Rachel Goodyear graduated in BA (hons) Fine Art at Leeds Metroplitan University in 2000, since which she has been practicing art in Manchester.

She has exhibited regularly in the UK and abroad including at The Drawing Room, at Tate Liverpool for The Liverpool Biennial, 2008; *The Intertwining Line*, The Cornerhouse, Manchester; *The Aesthetics of Anxiety*, Marc de Puechredon Gallery, Basel; and *ARTfutures*, Bloomberg Space, London. Her Solo projects include *Unable To Stop Because They Were Too Close To The Line*, commissioned by LIME (Pennine Arts Trust) and associated projects with Vital Arts and The Royal London Hospital; *Cats, Cold, Hunger and the Hostility of Birds*, a book of drawings published by Aye-Aye Books. In January 2009 Goodyear will present a collection of new works in her solo exhibition, *They Never Run, Only Call* at International 3, Manchester.

Rachel Goodyear is represented by International 3, Manchester, and Pippy Houldsworth, London.
w. *www.international3.com*
w. *www.houldsworth.co.uk*

24 — Rachel Goodyear

Q&A

What are you working on currently?

I have just exhibited a body of new work, *They Never Run, Only Call*, in January 2009 at the International 3, Manchester. It is a culmination of ideas I was working on for most of last year being stripped down to quite bleak, sometimes playful and occasionally nightmarish visions. This train of thought is continuing into another collection of mostly unseen drawings for my next exhibition at Houldsworth Gallery, London which opens in May 2009.

Whenever I begin a body of work I have no fixed idea as to what kind of characters or the nature of the thread will be, but it evolves over a period of time. It's an obsessive process, and it's at times like this that I notice changes in my work, and it can be quite precarious and intimidating. I have to keep questioning every drawing that I do, but still allow myself to go with the flow and see where it takes me.

Where did you study?

BA (Hons) Fine Art at Leeds Metropolitan University.

Who influenced your early years as an art student?

I was quite erratic at art college and over the three years tried different approaches to art making. During my foundation year I was inspired by Frida Kahlo for the colour and passion in her life in the face of adversity. Throughout college I had many books on Louise Bourgeois... My work was more sculptural and object based at the time, and was inspired by the emotional heavy weight of her environments and the ambitious scale, but also was drawn in to the mountainous volume of drawings that lie behind her work. I loved watching interviews with her. She mentioned at one time that she detested going to her own exhibition openings. At the time I felt cripplingly shy and self-conscious, and that response made me feel that I was somehow okay.

Have you ever seen, read about or heard of an artwork or art activity that made you think art could be significant?

At a time when I was finding the confidence that drawing was becoming the focus of my practice and coyly bringing my sketches out of my notebooks and into a public space, I remember two occasions that guided me further. In late 2002 a friend had returned from New York and brought back a catalogue from the MOMA exhibition, *Drawing Now — Eight Propositions*. I was so excited and inspired by what I saw on the pages, and intensely jealous that I couldn't see the actual show myself. Not long after that, another friend brought my attention to The Royal Art Lodge with a catalogue of their *Ask the Dust* exhibition, also in New York, at The Drawing Centre. The excitement I felt from leafing through these pages of such wonderful drawings certainly played a part in me finding my artistic identity after leaving college. I've closely followed the Royal Art Lodge's work ever since, and recently saw their exhibition at the Bluecoat for the Liverpool Biennial. They were beautiful, bleak and melancholic with a dark biting wit. Their images are still spinning round my mind.

Do you work on several things at once?

I tend to work on one drawing at a time, but there are always many ideas on the go in sketches and my mind at the same time. If there is an idea I can't quite capture I'll put it to one side, sometimes for a couple of weeks, sometimes a couple of years before returning to it. The environment of my studio is the opposite to my drawings. In contrast to the bleak, delicate and precise nature of my drawings, my studio is a frantic explosion of sketches, cuttings, writing, and ephemera. These are all things that I refer to every day I'm in the studio, so whilst I am focusing on one drawing there will be a whole load of other ideas and stories I'll be working through in my head, and sideline scribbles. In this way I often think of my work as being one big evolving drawing.

Do you enjoy making art?

I love drawing. It gives me equal pleasure and pain.

How do you deal with titles in your work?

Sometimes the title will simply refer to the protagonists in the picture or to an action I want to draw attention to, for example, *Girl and Dog*, or *Hypnotist*. At the same time, I collect phrases or collections of words lifted out of cuttings or conversations that lie around in notepads until an image arises that I feel marries up to it well. Examples of these are, *Unable to Stop Because They Were Too Close to the Line* and *The Birds Betrayed*. I guess my approach to titles is to not give too much away, or be as non-prescriptive as possible, or to add an extra bit of poetic ambiguity, to suggest a whole other part to the story off the page. I like to invite the viewer in to create their own narratives and build on the image they see in front of them in their own individual way, and titles can play such a huge part in this.

Where do you live/work?

I live and work in Manchester and Salford.

Why do you stay here?

I grew up just outside Manchester, but apart from my northern roots, I found Manchester was, from the outset, and still remains, a place where I want to practice art. There are very few alternative places I see myself living. When I first moved here I was very awkward and shy, but as I got involved in artist-run activity through volunteering and collaborative projects, I found it to be a really supportive city to work in. The city offered a 'give it a go' attitude, and I found it a great place to experiment and find my identity. I still feel it is a city I get a lot of support from and I still continue to enjoy living and making art here, and the music scene still throws up amazing things. I still feel I'm discovering new things and new people within the city. It's totally possible to be based and work in this city and operate on a national and international network.

What curators and galleries do you admire? Who are the biggest contributors to the art scene in the region?

For starters, International 3, in Manchester, and Pippy Houldsworth in London. They both represent me and have given me so much support. The Drawing Room in London, because they are dedicated to championing and exploring drawing as a practice in its widest sense and deliver inspiring exhibitions. Café Royal, a magazine and project run by Craig and Jo Atkinson, based in Liverpool, bringing together drawing through many different genres. Apartment, in Manchester, run by artists Paul Harfleet and Hilary Jack — right from the start they've presented great shows and interventions by local and international artists, and have a fantastic and supportive approach to curating, both from the gallery-in-domestic-space to offsite international collaborations.

I'd also like to champion my favourite place that can't just be classed just as a person, a gallery, a space or collective, but encompasses the whole lot. The Islington Mill, in Salford. It has always been a creative hub and has seen many changes through the years. It is owned by, and has been the vision of, Bill Campbell, and has played a huge part of in my life right from the week I moved here years ago. Under the umbrella of The Islington Mill Arts Club it encompasses studios with a glorious spectrum of creative practitioners — Bureau Gallery, The Islington Mill Arts Academy, events spaces and many on and offsite collective projects. I've seen it evolve over the years, and the attitude of 'can do' on the smallest or most ambitious of projects has been such an inspiration. Its eclectic mix brings together equally varied groups of people, and it's the kind of place you can see exhibitions of local and international artists, followed by film screenings, gigs from local talents such as Warm Widow and Lone Lady, exclusive performances by The Ting Tings and Acid Mother's Temple, spectacular visuals by photographer Andrew Brooks, jazz performance on a grand piano accompanied by the BBC philharmonic orchestra... the list is endless.

What are your plans for the future? If you had unlimited funds, what artwork would you make?

The notion of unlimited funds overwhelms me! If I could buy unlimited time with those funds that's what I'd do. I'm terrible at planning for the future as you never know what life throws at you, and with this your work can automatically change. My plans for the future are carrying on, seeing where it takes me and continuing to look for new inspiration.

If you could own any work of art, what would it be?

I've had a picture of Goya's *Don Manuel Osorio Manrique de Zuñiga* following me around for as long as I can remember. The well-known hauntingly-still image of the boy in a red suit with a magpie on a string with cats looking on from the shadows. I would happily settle for travel tickets to the Metropolitan Museum of Art to spend time with it.

I could also live in a Yayoi Kusama installation, and would love to live with anything by Amy Cutler, Peter Doig, Jockum Nordström or Raymond Pettibon to name a few.

If you weren't an artist what would you be doing?

I have often thought it would be amazing to be an entomologist. However, that would be a non-starter. I'm fascinated by all that creeps in the undergrowth, but have always had a deep-rooted terror of spiders.

Advice to new graduates?

Don't stop. Form a collective. Form a band. Exhibit in your house/shed/car/wherever.

Top Left
Eyeliner (2008). 30 x 42cm. Pencil and watercolour on paper. Private collection.

Far Left
Hypnotist (2008). 42 x 60cm. Pencil and watercolour on paper.

Left
Darkness coming (2008). 42 x 60cm. Pencil and watercolour on paper. Private collection.

Right
Bark stripped of its branches (2007). 30 x 42cm. Pencil and watercolour on paper. Private collection.

25 — Rachel Goodyear

Simon Le Ruez

Sheffield

Le Ruez at home.

Top
Pure Pleasure Seeker (2007). 77 x 77 x 15cm. MDF, foam, leather, knicker elastic, steel hanger. Courtesy of the artist and Vane Contemporary Art. © Simon Le Ruez. Photography Colin Davison.

Right
Chère Chérie (2008). 34 x 13 x 12cm. Leather, wax, oil paint, coloured rubber. Courtesy of the artist and Vane Contemporary Art. © Simon Le Ruez. Photography Simon Le Ruez.

Simon Le Ruez uses sculpture, installation, drawing and video, to construct a range of scenarios, incidents and seemingly random acts where meanings, like memories, need to be pieced together. He is interested in the things we are perhaps not meant to see, the forbidden intrigue of what goes on behind the net curtains, and recurring themes include that of longing and escape, unrequited or semi-fulfilled feelings and the suggestion of the places this may take us in order to seek a degree of relief. His work frequently refers to and oscillates between the notion of private domestic spaces and that of wide open metaphorical landscapes.

Interested in the junction between these instinctively contrasting places and how a complex narrative can unfold through a series, full of both emotional and aesthetic contradictions, Le Ruez's work frequently finds itself at a crossroads where the ordinary becomes slightly strange and where a subtle dose of unease is injected into the mundane.

In his sculptures, which are characterised by a disquieting and subversive use of materials such as lace, dried beans, copper piping, rubber, leather and knicker elastic he presents a string of unsettling scenarios which frequently conspire to create an air of erotic ambiguity and, very often, an underlying sense of humour. These materials, often brought together to suggest conflicting comforts, conjure a body of work that pivots around both physical and psychological tensions. The process of making, lies at the core of the work, and through a dialogue of little curiosities Le Ruez is interested in how the plight of individual lives and the rich layering of experience can be expressed through form.

Text courtesy of the artist

26 — Simon Le Ruez

Biog

Simon Le Ruez was born in Jersey in 1970 and currently lives and works in Sheffield, UK. He completed an MA in Sculpture at Winchester School of Art in 1995 and since then has exhibited widely both nationally and internationally.

Group exhibitions

The Golden Record, The Collection, Lincoln (2009); *Hidden Narratives*, Graves Art Gallery, Sheffield; *Anonymous Drawings*, Kunstraum Kreuzberg / Bethanien, Berlin (2008); *Rummage — Sculptors' Drawing*, Winchester Gallery, University of Southampton (2007); *Trajectory*, Leeds City Art Gallery, Leeds (2006).

Solo exhibitions

When the Quarry Calls, Vane, Newcastle upon Tyne, (2007); *Stories of Solitude*, Arhus Kunstbygning, Denmark; *Acts of Generosity*, Castlefield Gallery, Manchester (2005).

Vane Contemporary Art
e. info@vane.org.uk

Q&A

What are you working on currently?

I am currently working on a series of works under the generic title of *Colonia*. The series includes new sculptures, drawings, photographic and neon works. The starting point for this work comes from an article I read some time ago about a number of distinctive buildings on the coastline of northern Italy. Now abandoned and derelict, they were built as holiday hostels for the children of industrial workers who were members of the Fascist party. Constructed in the 1930's, these types of buildings were called a colonia, which literally translates as 'colony'. The hostels had utopian aspirations and their purpose was to promote health and fitness in an atmosphere of sun, sea and regular exercise within spectacular settings of modern architecture amid panoramic views. What fundamentally interested me, aside from the beauty of the abandoned buildings, was the notion of derelict utopias and the challenge of giving this notion form. I saw an arresting contradiction, in that, free of their intended strict regime with its underlying ugly agenda, these buildings now facing ruin projected a real beauty, not unlike characters who had lived a rich but sometimes turbulent life and who had a story to tell.

Aside from this I am working on some new film pieces, some which I can directly relate to the layering of concerns present within the *Colonia* body of work and another piece, 'The sins of Andre', which observes private pastimes. This is an empathetic portrait of André Mason, an elderly man who in his spare time immersed himself in a carved interpretation of the seven deadly sins.

Where did you study?

I studied in London and Winchester.

Who influenced your early years as an artist or art student?

My influences were varied early on, and remain so today. I saw many qualities in the work of Eva Hesse. I appreciated the tactility in the work, the play with materials and the fact that the work actually seemed to be saying something beyond this, something visceral. It made me aware of what was possible with sculpture. I also looked a lot at Franz Kline. His paintings were a kind of revelation for me. I liked the difficulties I felt with them but also the intensity. Robert Adams was someone I looked at early on, and he remains an important influence today. His photographs have always struck me as strange and austere. They operate on a number of levels, hinting at, yet refusing, narrative. I liked straight away the fact that I had to work as a viewer with his work to understand the level of experimentation, maturity and visual intelligence that was on offer. I would cite his monograph *The New West* as particularly influential.

Have you ever seen, read about or heard of an artwork or art activity (other than your own) that made you think art could be significant?

A lot of what Duchamp did struck me as significant because he saw the need at a particular time for deconstruction, liberation and rewriting the rules. Some of Joseph Beuys's actions are hugely significant because for me they remain fresh and relevant. His work *I Like America and America Likes Me* (1974) is astounding in its ambition. With this work he managed to create something consistently visually interesting over a three-day period and simultaneously raise some politically poignant questions. He was an incredibly versatile artist and this work was another example of what art could be and what it could do.

In more recent times Rachel Whiteread's (1993), the cast of the inside of a Victorian house in the East End of London, had significance because it became (albeit for a brief period) a public work of art that really got a wide demographic of people talking. The most interesting thing for me about this work was its context, how it challenged the notion of boring and predictable public works of art sited in front of grand or not so grand buildings or in parks, and the questions it raised about the nature and definition of beauty.

Do you work on several things at once?

I am always working on several things at once. Aside from it being in my nature to be quite obsessive about things and it being useful to turn to something else when I recognise this, I like to try to get a dialogue going between works, to create an exchange or a kind of awkward conversation, and having different works on the go is conducive to this.

Do you enjoy making art?

Most of the time I enjoy it. I go through occasional battles where there is any number of places I would prefer to be than in the studio, but thankfully these tend to pass quite quickly. When things are going well and I recognise that the work is progressive I can feel a kind of euphoria.

How do you deal with titles in your work?

Titles have always been very important to me, to a point where I see them as an extension of the work. I have 'post it' notes all over my studio with little phrases on them that I have heard on the radio or read in a book and they tend to haunt me as potential titles. I see titling as another form of play and something that I shouldn't have to work too hard at; when I have found myself doing this it is when a work is left Untitled.

Where do you live/work?

I live and work in Sheffield.

What is it like to live and work here?

I have lived and worked here for eight years now, and I sort of gravitated here as it felt like a less obvious place for an artist in the UK to be than in London. There is a healthy cultural side to the city, with some interesting spaces and a diverse range of artists, and as I like the outdoors one can easily escape for long walks in the Peak District.

Why do you stay here?

I stay because at the moment I don't have to make too many compromises. I get to spend a decent amount of time making work, and I know that that might be a harder thing to achieve in another city. Also there are things that still surprise and amuse me here. The moment that stops it may be time to be somewhere else.

Who or what has made the biggest contribution to the contemporary art scene in the region?

I think there are some key, dynamic individuals who have instigated spaces and initiatives that has given a platform for work and simultaneously offered tangents and texture to the contemporary art scene. I would also have to extend a nod to the Arts Council for their support of individual artists, a few of which have gone on to realise strong bodies of work and present some great shows.

Who else should we be watching?

Out of artists working in the North, I like Rachel Goodyear's drawings; the work seems to be consistently interesting and inventive. Maud Haya-Baviera, a French artist based in Sheffield, is one to watch. Working with film, photography and drawing her work is often imbued with cinematic and literary reference points, which she cleverly reinterprets in surprising ways.

What curators and galleries do you admire and why (locally or internationally)?

In the UK I admire Matt's Gallery in London and its founder Robin Klassnik because of his genuine agenda to support the experimental side of an artists practice. I have seen some important shows at the gallery, and they work with some fascinating artists who include Mike Nelson and Fiona Crisp. The Henry Moore Institute in Leeds frequently stages some fantastic exhibitions; it's a seductive space, and the display of work is always meticulous. Away from the UK, I have seen some courageous shows at KW Institute for Contemporary Art, in Berlin. It is a space that seems to have wide parameters in what it is prepared to show.

What are your plans for the future? If you had unlimited funds, what artwork would you make?

My plans are to continue to aspire to make strong work. I think it is important to make work that is relevant, but to always pursue an individualistic resolve. It is the clearest way forward for me, and my hope to leave fingerprints somewhere. I would like to diversify my practice to incorporate a wider tableau. I tend to see the sculptural potential in most art forms and I love materials and their possibilities, but I am intrigued by the discipline of film and video at the moment and maybe this medium is going to play a greater part in things. As for having unlimited funds, right now, I would indulge in the realisation of a series of text-based neon pieces. I would also like to play with scale a lot more and create a number of large derelict utopias the viewer could experience from the inside and outside. Perhaps some of the neon pieces would work on the inside of these, at the end of ambiguously constructed passageways.

If you could own any work of art, what would it be?

It's incredibly hard to pin it down to just one but it would be a toss up between Douglas Gordon's film *Between Darkness and Light* (1997) and Louise Bourgeois' *Red Rooms* (1994). I saw the Gordon piece for the first time as part of his retrospective in Avignon over the summer, and it was the most affecting work I have experienced for some time.

If you weren't an artist, what job would you like/rather be doing?

I like gardening, which dovetails neatly with my aforementioned love of the outdoors, so that would certainly be an option.

Do you have any advice for this year's graduates?

It can take a long time to find an interesting language but in the meantime it is important to keep working and seeing work. Ambition is necessary, but it is more important to have ambition for the work.

Freee

Sheffield / Hull / Warrington

Freee is a collective made up of three artists, Dave Beech, Andy Hewitt and Mel Jordan, who work together on slogans, billboards and publications that challenge the commercial and bureaucratic colonisation of the public sphere of opinion formation. They occupy the public sphere with works that take sides, speak their mind and divide opinion.

They are currently artists in residence for Groundwork in Dartington, developing a critical utopian response to the merger of Dartington College with Falmouth University.

Spin[Freee]oza, commissioned by Skor, for SMART Project Space's exhibition On Joy, Sadness and Desire 9 May — 28 June 2009, created a mini-public sphere in Amsterdam via a dozen shop windows, a thousand sloganeering balloons, three billboards and a pamphlet. Freee entered into a debate on democracy and dissensus with slogans such as 'knowledge cannot check power by being true, but only by being converted into agency', published in vinyl text on shop windows, in turn used as backgrounds for billboard print photos of the artists, and later as the route for gallery-visitors to carry their free balloons home.

Freee is interested in the traffic between the gallery and the street, between art's institutions and everyday culture, and between art and politics. Sharing and contesting opinion through acts of publishing is central to all of Freee projects. Making ideas public by printing, publishing and disseminating slogans is the first step of a dissensual public practice for a counter-public sphere. The artists take it that this sort of questioning is essential for any democracy worthy of the name.

Text courtesy of Freee

Top
Protest Drives History, May (2008). Poster. Commissioned for ICA Bar for Nought to Sixty exhibition. (June – November 2008). Photography Catherine Hyland.

Right
Advertising For All; Or For Nobody At All; Reclaim Public Opinion (2009). Billboard poster. ICA, London. Photography Lotte Juul Petersen.

28 — Freee

Biog

Solo Exhibitions

2008 How to be Hospitable, Collective Gallery, Edinburgh
2005 The Neo-Imperialist Function, Second Guangzhou Triennale, Guangzhou, China
2005 What are aesthetics?, Ponte dei Barcaroli, Venice Biennale, Venice, Italy

Group Exhibitions

2007 Peace Camp, Brick Lane Gallery, London
2006 Have you heard the one about the public sphere?, commissioned by Hull Time Based Arts, Hull
2005 The Regeneration Function, at the London in Six Easy Steps exhibition, ICA, London
2004 Futurology: The Black Country 2024, New Art Gallery, Walsall

Public commissions

2006 How to talk to public art, BBC and Arts Council England commission for the Power of Art, International 3, Manchester, UK

w. *www.freee.org.uk*

Q&A

What are you working on currently?

We are interested in advertising and so, at the moment, we are occupying billboard sites in order to 'not' advertise anything; for example, a recent slogan we wrote, *Advertising wants to convert our desire for a better life into a desire to buy something*. This is a work that occupies the place of an advert on a commercial billboard site, only to propose a total reconfiguration of advertising. We are thinking about the gap between the utopian promises of liberal consumerism and the harsh reality of neo-liberal market forces.

Advertisements have become a prominent feature of public space and the public sphere. No consideration of popular culture, urban experience, economic, the public sphere or art's social context can ignore their existence. Advertising is, in effect, the perfect public sphere for a society geared toward consumption, markets and profit. This means that advertising is always an advert for capitalism in general before it is an advert for any product in particular. As an industry, and as individual campaigns, advertising is at once made possible by capitalism and crushed by it. As such, it is not only our desire for a better life that is redirected into purchases, it is advertising itself that is ruined for the sake of sales.

The radical response, however, is not to obliterate advertising, not to reform it. Advertising in its current form is entirely embedded in contemporary capitalism. It is only the abolition of capitalism that can bring about the kind of shift in advertising that Freee are calling for. This is why in another recent work called *Everyone is a Guerilla Advertiser (after the revolution)*, this time as a video, we produced a string of mini-protest performances in Trafalgar Square. We have also written a new Manifesto entitled, *The Freee Manifesto of Guerilla Advertising (after the revolution)*.

So we are producing billboards that propose billboards as a counter-advertisement. It is an attempt to imagine advertising as available to everyone, not an industry monopolised by big business. Our images carry a slogan, but they also carry an implicit message: 'everyone is or can be a guerilla advertiser'.

Advertising that engages in a political critique of advertising and the society that requires advertising to survive, is advertising for another world.

Where did you study and how did you meet?

Mel's a cockney, Andy's from Hull, and Dave is from Warrington. We got to know each other as students, Dave and Mel met at Leicester Polytechnic. Some years later Dave and Andy met when studying in London at the RCA, and Mel and Andy met when they worked in Sheffield. Mel and Andy worked together for several years and they began working with Dave in 2004 when they were all teaching together at Wolves. We have all worked together ever since.

Who influenced your early years as artist or as art students?

We liked 1960's conceptualists, like Vito Acconci, Allan Kaprow, Art & Language, Robert Barry and later conceptual-inspired artists such as Jeff Koons.

Have you ever seen, read about or heard of an artwork or art activity (other than your own) that made you think art could be significant?

Yes, regularly. We like Mark McGowan's work. Recently, for example, he did a re-enactment of the conception of Prince William, and he has run a series of campaigns about issues he wants to promote. He has campaigned to save the great British breakfast — one of our favourite works is where he walks backwards wearing a T-shirt that states 'This is not a protest'. He courts the media beautifully, and they want to cover his work because McGowan's campaigns are extraordinary or controversial or both, so the media want to pan his art as a way of panning art generally. McGowan gives art a bad name, and we think that's great; he contests the idea that art is natural, normal, civilising and good for everyone.

Do you work on several things at once?

Yes, we are always busy and juggling a number of projects at the same time, like most people.

Do you enjoy making art?

Not sure that we enjoy it in the same way that we enjoy other activities like leisure — going to the cinema, et cetera, but we are committed to working at it, developing an enquiry and testing ideas.

How do you deal with titles in your work?

Our works are slogans. We write slogans... the slogan is always the title. We write what we believe in. We don't believe in works without titles.

Where do you live/work?

Sheffield and London and work all over the place with collaborators and supporters.

Who or what has made the biggest contribution to the contemporary art scene in this region?

Arts Council England Yorkshire — funding! Activity on the ground — grass roots — No Fixed Abode in Sheffield, Black Dogs in Leeds, Salford Restoration Office, small organizations set up by people who have firm commitments to developing new ways of working through the problems in art. International 3.

Who else should we be watching?

Plastique Fantastique; Hut Project; Carey Young — always; Gail Pickering — mad fantastic stuff; Mark Hutchinson...

What curators and galleries do you admire, and why (locally or internationally)?

Andy Hunt is a terrific curator who has just become the director of Focal Point Gallery in Southend-on-sea, he is someone to watch. Andy puts his money where his mouth is by working with artists who have something to say and really supporting them. He's got to be one of the UK's most interesting curators.

Gavin Wade at Eastside Projects, in Birmingham, has got a new space and really knows how to put on an exciting show. He loves collaborating with people, and produces masses of new work like no one else.

Paul O'Neill works out of Situations, in Bristol, and he is very interesting for us; we were part of his *Coalesce show* which opened at SMART in Amsterdam, in January 2009.

Also Hilde de Bruijn, at SMART, has a brilliant programme. Richard Birkett was great during the *Nought to Sixty* show at the ICA, London, and he has asked us to do another poster for the café — which will be up in February 2009. And we love the way curators like Pete Lewis and Esther Windsor work.

We are about to do a project (September 2009) with Lotte Juul Petersen at Wysing Arts Centre. She is great fun and nothing feels like a problem, so we are looking forward to working with her. International 3 in Manchester are very supportive of our work.

What are your plans for the future? If you had unlimited funds, what artwork would you make?

As long as we have these questions running round our heads we will keep working, so I guess that will be for some time to come. It would be great to have more funds, as it allows you to think about altering your production and to be more ambitious with the scale or number of works you produce. We are thinking about advertising at the moment. As you might have seen we often use billboards for our slogans, so if we had more money we might look at competing with the advertising industry and running some campaigns across a range of media. We would really like to take over all the billboards in one town and free a place up from advertising for two weeks to see what it felt like! Or maybe running a TV channel?

If you could own any work of art, what would it be?

Any of these... A can of Manzoni's shit, a Vito Acconci building, Daniel Buren painting in a cardboard box, a Jeff Koons balloon work, a video work by Mark McGowan — McGowan appearing on TV news. I like the fact that conceptual work is something you can own in your head — a good idea is something you can just imagine — and you don't need to own it, I prefer to go and buy a gorgeous pair of shoes instead. Please note, it was Andy that said that!

If you weren't an artist group, what job would you rather be doing?

We like being an artist group because we like working together, its great to work collectively and do something you believe in.

Do you have any advice for this year's graduates?

I only have advice for those artists who want to change the world, the others can fuck off! We've always had an antagonistic relationship to art, as it is a minority form of culture — hence our desire to destroy it. We'd like young artists to change art, and change society at the same time, so that's our advice. Don't look to us for tips on your art career, but if you're interested in dissent, we'd be glad to help – email us!

29 — Freee

Matthew Houlding

Todmorden

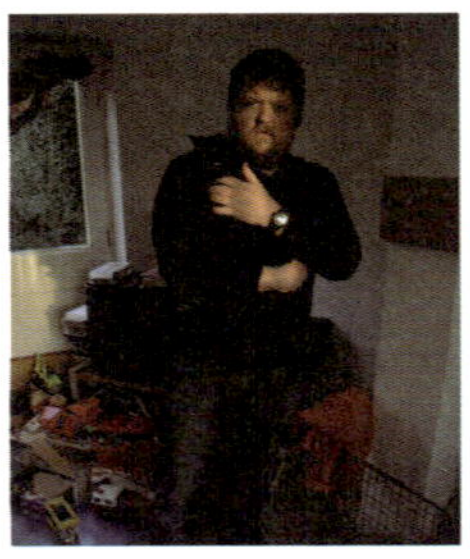

Houlding at home.

Top
Department of Housing and Leisure [Blue] (2008). 300mm x 420mm. Montage. Photography courtesy of Ceri Hand Gallery.

Right
Mistral (2007). 800 x 550 x 700mm. Mixed media. Photography courtesy of Buro Fur Kunst.

Matthew Houlding takes the idea of the architect's model but subverts both the material and the function, taking us on an adventure into uncharted territory. The works celebrate the idea of concept architecture and the pursuit of personal utopian ideals.

Houldings' works summon desire and hope, intricately constructed from disparate found materials gathered over time: cardboard packaging, weathered timber, found postcards and colour photocopies from forgotten books on holidays, all of which have landscapes written into their surfaces, reminding us that everything and everyone has the potential for another life.

With a wonderful feeling for material, Houlding shifts meanings and creates new forms. In addition to his critique of architecture he creates dreams of spaces and backdrops for stories and new ideas, neither of yesterday nor of tomorrow, but set in a time of their own.

Houlding's art is dedicated to a synthesis of art, design and architecture, a belief that art is capable of leading humankind to a brighter future. It offers models of thought, inviting us to reflect on our experience and environment and unveils our longing to retreat to a man-made haven.

Text courtesy of the artist ▸ Continued on page 35

Biog

Matthew Houlding was born in Keighley in 1966 and lives and works in Todmorden, West Yorkshire. He has exhibited widely in the UK and Europe and is represented by Büro Für Kunst, Dresden, Galerie Elly Brose-Eiermann, Berlin, and Ceri Hand Gallery, Liverpool.

e. info@cerihand.co.uk
e. galerie@ellybroseeiermann.de

Q&A

Top Left
Heartbreaker (2008). Mixed media. 550mm x 350mm x 400mm Photography James Alderson.

Top Right
Pacific Swiss (2007). Mixed media. 1100mm x 600mm x 700mm. Photography courtesy of Buro Fur Kunst.

Lower Left
Independent Workshop (2008). Montage. 300 x 420mm. Photography courtesy of Ceri Hand Gallery.

Lower Right
Amaryllis [overview] (2008). Mixed media. In 4 parts: North, South, East, West. Dimensions of each approx 1800 x 500 x 800mm. Photography Simon Pantling.

What are you working on currently?
  Work for shows at Ceri Hand Gallery and ArtGene.
Where did you study?
  Loughborough College of Art & Design.
Who influenced your early years as an artist or art student?
  Picasso, Joseph Beuys and the Bauhaus.
Have you ever seen, read about or heard of an artwork or art activity (other than your own) that made you think art could be significant?
  De Stijl and the Bauhaus.
Do you work on several things at once?
  Yes
Do you enjoy making art?
  Most of the time.
How do you deal with titles in your work?
  As seriously as possible — they are part of the work.
Where do you live / work?
  Todmorden, West Yorkshire.
What is it like to live and work here?
  You have good times and you have bad times.
Why do you stay here?
  Because you can escape here and no-one follows. It's easy and logistically it is very good.
Who or what has made the biggest contribution to the contemporary art scene in this region? Who else should we be watching?
  Stuart Edmondson, David Cochrane.
What curators and galleries do you admire and why, locally or internationally?
  Richard Hylton. Unit 2 Gallery, London. Kaavous Clayton.
What are your plans for the future/If you had unlimited funds, what artwork would you make?
  Build a boat and a house and live in Zanzibar.
If you could own any work of art, what would it be?
  A Bigger Splash by David Hockney.
If you weren't an artist, what job would you like/rather be doing?
  Boat builder
Do you have any advice for this years graduates?
  Beware of procrastination.

35 — Matthew Houlding

Rory Macbeth

Leeds

Macbeth in his studio.

Ever since inventing a student at Central St Martin's foundation, who, fully enrolled, existed purely in admin and rumour, and who passed the course with a portfolio gleaned at the last minute from bins, I have sought to unpick our assumptions about what actually seems to be around us. The clash of reality with ideals, of language with the real world, and a constant sense of disappointment with what things claim and what they deliver, have been my ongoing inspiration. The work aims to undo our expectations of what is around us, and cajoles and sometimes tricks the audience into being complicit in the work.

Biog

Rory Macbeth is an artist working in Leeds and London, and has shown nationally and internationally in a variety of commercial and non-commercial spaces, including the Nassauischer Kunstverein, Wiesbaden; V1 Gallery, Copenhagen; Tate Britain; Laden fuer Nichts, Leipzig; Northern Gallery for Contemporary Art, Sunderland; and Galerie Sara Guedj, Paris, who represents him. He is also the founder and co-director of PILOT, the only large-scale international forum and archive of artists who are not represented by galleries.

36 — Rory Macbeth

Q&A

Top Left
Tree (2005). 6m x 3m x 2mm. Cut leaves. Courtesy of the artist and Galerie Sara Guedj.

Left Middle
Respray [Piaggio, Metalic Pink] (2004). Burned-out scooter, spray paint. Photography Colin Guillemet. Courtesy of the artist and Galerie Sara Guedj.

Left Bottom
Statue [Hamlet's fag break] (2007). Wax, fibreglass, paint, clothes, hair, found objects. Courtesy of Leif Djurhuus and Galerie Sara Guedj.

What are you working on currently?

I'm translating a Kafka novel into English from German (I think). I don't speak the language, so it's really hard work — just staring at sentences till they make sense. It's starting to create it's own narrative, which is odd. I thought it would just be a jumble of nonsense. I want to make it into an audio book, and I've got it in my head that the actor, Robert Powell, should read it.

I'm also getting a marching band to re-enact something I stumbled across in Switzerland, and also to play a piece where they all sustain a note of as long as possible (up to forty-five seconds for a cornet player, apparently!). I'm pulping books in a food-mixer with water, and pouring them out into spillages that dry. The books are seminal moments in human understanding (it all sounds a bit thuggish, but won't be, I hope). I'm pretending to paint abstract paintings on top of second-hand landscape paintings for a pretend abstract show. I'm looking at crash barriers for a piece, and I'm about to carve another tree out of wood... a bit of a Casper David Friedrich-type tree, hopefully. I'm involved in a collaborative project with Amy Stephens at the moment. It's part of a really wrong-footed show where artists are randomly paired-up to make work together. In my experience, collaboration never really works like that, so with a bit of luck something really odd might emerge from the attempt. I'm also repairing old work that has got damaged (I seem to do this a lot). This time it is a waxwork of one of those buskers who pretend to be a statue on the street. She took a bit of a tumble in a Museum in Denmark, and most of her fingers snapped off, and her nose is squashed.

Where did you study?

I first studied at Edinburgh University (basically an English Literature course with bits of art history, æsthetics, and philosophy thrown in), but the degree that was really useful was Fine Art at Central Saint Martins, London.

Who influenced your early years as an artist or art student?

Before I ever thought about doing art, I saw some documentaries about Christo, Andy Warhol and Chris Burden that have stuck a bit, and I remember seeing some early YBA stuff that intrigued me... But more than anything, I was influenced by the people I studied with, who had an infectious thirst for knowledge that engendered a sense that we could do anything we wanted. I was also really influenced by a lot of stuff I found really bad or misguided... I think pulling that stuff apart was as important to my understanding as anything... and there was a lot of bad stuff in London at the time, as well as good. It's a great combination, especially if you see lots of it.

Have you ever seen, read about or heard of an artwork or art activity (other than your own) that made you think art could be significant?

Lots. I'm not sure how to begin listing them. More than any single work, *Tristram Shandy* by Laurence Sterne has always stood out as a beacon of possibilities, and a breathtaking achievement, but alongside that Titian, Fra Angelico, Kevin Rowland, *Andrei Rublev* by Tarkovsky, Spike Milligan, Velázquez. There's too many. That's what I'm thinking today... tomorrow it'll be different, but with Sterne still there at the top, probably.

Do you enjoy making art?

I love making art.

How do you deal with titles in your work?

Not very well... I find it really hard... I always want my titles to have some kind of depth and mystery or poetry about them, and they always end up being pedantically descriptive. But if that's what happens then there's at least some kind of honesty in their blandness, perhaps. Or sometimes they're just crap linguistic jokes.

Where do you live / work?

I live in Leeds. I've got two studios at the moment, which sounds very grand, but isn't really. One is a communal studio I helped set up in the old Limehouse Town Hall in London, which is an event space (it's a ballroom!) and open-remit studio, which is a bit of a one-of-a-kind set up, and which is very close to my heart. I'm using it more for meetings, and as a storage and shipping point, at the moment, though I make stuff there from time to time. Most of my work is being done in my studio in Leeds, which is in a business park — exactly the opposite of the London space, but with it's own weirdness going on... being sandwiched between a call-centre and a testing facility that has sunshine machines!

What is it like to live and work here?

Living is pretty straightforward, but I really struggled working in Leeds at first, as it was so different to everything I'd surrounded myself with in London. But you sort of adjust, and make it work. I'm not sure I'm fully acclimatised yet, so I can't really answer. I wouldn't have been able to answer that about London even after ten years, so maybe I'll only be able to answer this if I leave Leeds.

Why do you stay here?

Pragmatics. I can just about support my family (we've just had a son) up here, on my limited earnings, which just wouldn't have worked in London. My girlfriend is from Leeds, so we moved up to have the baby, and then ended up staying

Who or what has made the biggest contribution to the contemporary art scene in the region?

Annoyingly, in some ways it seems London has made one of the biggest contributions, in that it has traditionally drained a good deal of talent away, and everything seems to have been answerable to it. But that seems to be changing now, so perhaps now and in the near future a real optimism and exciting sense of ambition, along with a generosity of spirit, are what will make the biggest contribution

Who else should we be watching?

There are a whole bunch of young artists in Leeds who seem to be really active and thoughtful and adventurous, all loosely associated around set-ups like The Art Market, the sprawling Black Dogs collective and Nous Vous. But there's more too, most of which seems to just be just starting to bubble up... this groundswell seems to have a good energy to it.

What curators and galleries do you admire and why (locally or internationally)?

On the whole I don't find that much to admire in galleries, other than being good businesses, so it's a bit like asking me what my favourite manufacturing industries are. There are some exceptions that I've stumbled across. I think that really interesting galleries are ones that are re-evaluating the structure they work in, like the Berlin model of gallery whereby a group of like-minded artists get a space and pay a gallerist to represent them. That's a fairly basic shift in power relations that sort of works, but there are better new models emerging. There's a shift in the power of art fairs too, and I think we're not a long way off some commercial galleries not having a shop front, but existing only in Art Fairs. This would really make sense for a city like Leeds, which can't sustain a commercial contemporary art gallery in the traditional sense, but has great contemporary artists to represent. Anyhow, here's some I like for a variety of reasons...

Maes & Matthys Gallery (Antwerp). They are a commercial gallery that use some of their profits to pay a wage to artists like Vaast Colson, who are brilliant, but don't really make anything particularly saleable. They are recognising that a gallery gets far more from an artist than a cash transaction. This is not only a great gesture culturally, but a really intelligent business strategy that will stand them in much better stead than the standard selling strategies of most galleries.

Galerie Sara Guedj (Paris). A (really) young gallery that represent me, and whose lack of experience, honesty, infectious excitement and intelligence I really warmed to.

V1 (Copenhagen). Seem to be riding a bit of a wave, but behind the trendy coolness of where they are at, there is a warmth and straightforwardness in their approach. They are happy to not always get it quite right, which I think is really important.

V22 (London). I've never met them, but they seem to have been trying some really interesting alternative models of funding and self-sufficiency that don't rely on the market or funding in the traditional sense. They have become a public limited company, and created a collection in which artists and collector-patrons own shares... ha-ha... I just nicked that bit from their website to make it sound like I know what I'm talking about... but you get the idea.

As to curators, there are so many around. Everyone's having a go (it's like everyone being a DJ in the 90's). I always admired BANK's iconoclastic approach, but equally admire curators when you don't get any sense of them being involved at all. I'm always attracted to people pushing the possibilities of curating a bit, like Robert Blackson doing a show of smells, or Eleanor Brown's curated newspapers.

What are your plans for the future? If you had unlimited funds, what artwork would you make?

One project I am currently working on is a Festival of Curating. There are generations of curators being pumped out by courses all over the world, but there is no large-scale event to properly examine and debate curating. Much of what curators do is weirdly under the radar, and the idea would be to examine the variety of curatorial approaches with a fresh transparency. The event will be in a tower block with one or two curators in identical spaces on each floor (fifteen to twenty in all), all producing a show that somehow is a statement of their agenda. A visitor would be able to make a comparative study of approaches of curators from a worldwide variety of backgrounds, have lunch in a café halfway up, and a beer at the top!

If you could own any work of art, what would it be?

I don't really feel compelled to own artwork really, but I'd have no complaints living with the weirdness of a detail from some pre-renaissance Italian fresco or a van der Weyden.

If you weren't an artist what job would you like/rather be doing?

I really can't imagine. It took me fifteen years to find this one.

Do you have any advice for this year's graduates?

Prove us wrong.

37 — Rory Macbeth

Paul Rooney

Liverpool

Rooney at home.

I currently make text, sound and video works that focus on the 'voices' of semi-fictional personas which are presented as written, sung or spoken monologues. The works have as their basis the nature of individual subjectivity and identity in relation to place and history, and they focus in particular on the difficulty of attempting to render historical memory in language or art. All of the works use or reference narrative forms such as short stories, songs, audio guides and letters.

The narratives voiced by the personas — a hotel maid, a packaging company middle-manager, an airborne sprite — sometimes start from a real interview with a real person or group of people, but are as likely to arise from a scene from a novel, a TV documentary or an overheard local urban myth. Each voice is not presented as a unified identity but as a collection of many different voices or cultural and historical references, and all of the separate sources that are referenced in the monologues, including the interviews, are not treated as authentic or inviolable, but are often extended into fiction or used mischievously.

I try to allow each piece I make to filter different ideas through the persona involved. A short story I published recently explored a comedian's ambition for his writing, and his willingness to literally erase himself to fulfill the potential he felt that his writing had. A recent sound work extended the Brecht/Weill song 'Pirate Jenny' into a hotel maid's meditation on the presence of history within the everyday; and a new 16mm film I am working on, based on a packaging company manager's trip to Paris, in May 1968, engages with the subjective experience of contemporary events as often one of distance rather than engagement.

There are moments in the works when we suddenly glimpse into a world of unsettling absurdity or ambiguity, and these moments, triggered by comically odd twists in the narrative or by the visual or musical context, are crucial to the understanding of the work as a whole. These moments can create a shift in perspective, revealing how our mundane and routine world also resonates with constellations of historical presences, unfulfilled potentials and the messiness of our subjective experience. I am also interested, however, in the fact that we can only get anywhere near presenting these complexities in art if we acknowledge the formal nature of that art.

Biog

Artist Paul Rooney was born in Liverpool in 1967, and trained at Edinburgh College of Art. Paul's practice focused from 1997 to 2000 on the music of the 'Rooney' CDs and performances. Rooney achieved an appearance in John Peel's *Festive Fifty* in 1998, and a 'Peel session' in 1999.

Paul has had residencies at Dundee Contemporary Arts/University of Dundee VRC; Proyecto Batiscafo, Cuba; Tate Liverpool (MOMART Fellowship); and was the ACE Oxford-Melbourne Artist Fellow for 2004. Paul has shown recently in group projects at Tate Britain, London; Museo Nacional Centro de Arte Reina Sofia, Madrid; Kunst-Werke Berlin, Berlin; the Shanghai Biennial; Tate Liverpool; and in *British Art Show 6*, which toured around the UK in 2005-2006. Paul has had solo shows at Matt's Gallery, London, and Collective Gallery, Edinburgh, in 2008.

Other recent projects include a 12" red vinyl record broadcast on Radio Lancashire, Radio 1 and BBC 6 Music, a video for Film and Video Umbrella touring to fourteen cities around Europe, and a short story published by Serpent's Tail. Paul was the winner of the second Northern Art Prize in 2008.

Q&A

What are you working on currently?

At the moment I am working on a book with artist John Holden, for which I am writing a short story involving vampires living in a Turkish holiday resort, that should be out at the end of the 2009; and I am also working on a video project for a show linked to the 100th anniversary of the death of the English writer Malcolm Lowry, which will be at the Bluecoat Gallery in autumn, 2009. Hopefully, the video will tour to another venue also.

The outline synopsis of the video at the moment (this is early stage, so the final work may be very different to this) is that the main character, Bill, a frazzled alcoholic journalist, wakes from his nap in the middle of a meeting of a focus group arranged by an advertising firm, which is using the conference facilities of a beautiful English stately home. It seems (though nothing is obviously clear, and takes time to unravel) that though Bill is, in reality, taking part in the focus group, in his head he is living out a fantasy world arising out of his obsession with Malcolm Lowry. Bill apparently believes he is an English writer and failed jazz musician staying in a 1930's New York psychiatric institution (as did Lowry). This world overtakes Bill's conscious perception to the point that other members of the focus group become characters in his disorientating fantasy, though the context and the actors' dress mostly remains that of the modern day.

This new work will extend my interest in the artifice of narrative construction, and how artifice is all we have to make sense of the world. As with previous work I have done, I will adapt a pre-existing text, the Malcolm Lowry story 'Lunar Caustic', and re-write and develop it in a new context. I am interested in language play, how differing 'voices' — such as contemporary marketing speak or mid-20th Century literary Modernism — can be deliberately disrupted through collision to emphasise both their deceit and their formal delight. The work will reveal the division between what we believe to be real and the power of our own imaginative worlds to be not as clear as we think it is.

Where did you study?

Southport College of Art Foundation course, 1985-86, and Edinburgh College of Art, 1986-1991.

Who influenced your early years as an artist or art student?

I went through a few phases: Oscar Kokoschka and related Expressionism at foundation course; RB Kitaj, Édouard Manet, Walter Benjamin, James Joyce, Samuel Beckett at art college. Hard to say how the literary stuff I was into influenced my work, though, as I was making paintings, but now fiction writing has become part of my practice.

Have you ever seen, read about or heard of an artwork or art activity (other than your own) that made you think art could be significant?

I'll never forget reading a review of the John Cale album, *Music For A New Society*, in a 1983 NME, and I then went out and bought it on the strength of the review (without hearing the record at all, which I had never done before). The review used phrases like 'barbaric beauty', or similar. Can't remember exact quotes from it or who wrote it, but the album is still one of the best I have ever heard. I also remember seeing a Joy Division video on Saturday morning children's TV in 1980 (I was twelve) and having a profound reaction to it, a feeling akin to suddenly realising what art was, though I didn't conceptualise it like that at the time, of course.

Do you work on several things at once?

It depends what needs to be done, but ideally two works is the most I can do at one time, as my works are quite long and complicated now.

Do you enjoy making art?

I hate starting a work, it's never easy and you always have to put it off until you can't put it off anymore, but once the work is up and running it's great.

How do you deal with titles in your work?

I usually use a line or phrase from the text within the work itself, such as a line from the script, then you can avoid trying to sum the work up in the title.

Where do you live/work?

I write and research in my house in Liverpool. The filming or sound recording I do happens wherever it has to happen.

What is it like to live and work here?

It's as good and bad as anywhere else, I'm sure. I try to make a living out of making art, so I need to be in a place that's well resourced but still affordable. Most of the things I need to make work are here, I was able to afford to buy a house here a few years ago and you can still park for free near Liverpool city centre. The fact that Liverpool is a depopulated city means you can have a feeling of loads of space without too many people cluttering it up.

Why do you stay here?

I don't have a particular loyalty to the North West even though a lot of my work is based around stories or places in the area. Although, thinking about it, those works are quite numerous, so maybe I have. I'm sure if I still lived in Scotland the work would refer to Scottish contexts, it just depends where you find yourself. My family are here (I am from Liverpool originally, my partner is from Scotland) so it's great for our two-year-old to see at least one side of his family regularly; his cousin, auntie and nan and grandad. And it's still quite cheap to live here. I have considered other options of places to be but they have all been ruled out because of expense or language problems, or the positives don't beat the family proximity benefits of Liverpool.

Who, or what, has made the biggest contribution to the contemporary art scene in this region?

It's hard to think of anyone who has made as big or as long-standing a contribution as Bryan Biggs at The Bluecoat in Liverpool. I was in a Christmas show there in 1990 and have had a lot of support from the Bluecoat since then, but Bryan has been supporting countless Liverpool artists since the early eighties and is still doing it.

Who else should we be watching?

There are a number of very good artists based in the North West. A few I could mention that live in Liverpool are Leo Fitzmaurice, David Jacques, Harry Lawson, Brendan Lyons, Richard Proffitt, Imogen Stidworthy, Kai-Oi Jay Yung.

What curators and galleries do you admire (locally or internationally)?

Robin Klassnik at Matt's Gallery in London has an amazing record of showing and supporting some of the best (and sometimes most 'unfashionable') artists around, over many years. Camden Art Centre has had a very good run of shows recently, including Matthew Buckingham, the Steven Claydon-curated show, and Aernout Mik.

What are your plans for the future? If you had unlimited funds, what artwork would you make?

Plans for the future, see Question 1. I can't see further ahead than the works that I'm doing at the moment. Exhibitions-wise, one other North West thing to mention is a new solo show I am doing at Storey Gallery, Lancaster, from end of August 2009, after it re-opens following refurbishment. It will be nice to show a collection of work done in the last few years that hasn't been shown together before.

I would hope, if I had unlimited resources, I would make the work I am making now. I try to do what I want to do, and find the resources to do it. Having said all that, I'm sure having unlimited resources would distort my practice somehow. It's hard to know without giving it a go!

If you could own any work of art, what would it be?

A little Cy Twombly work on paper would be nice.

If you weren't an artist, what job would you like/rather be doing?

Artist is choice number one, number two would be a job involving reading books for a living without any strings attached. If such a job existed.

Do you have any advice for this year's graduates?

If you want to be an artist stick at it, keep going. If you want to do it enough, you will be able to keep going, if you don't you won't. In the end you need to get enough pleasure from the practice of making work to sustain you, because nothing else, no career successes or setbacks, will keep you keeping on if you don't do it for the shear love of doing it.

Top Left
Paul Rooney (2008).
'La Décision Doypack'
(production still).
27 minute 16mm film transferred to DVD.

Top Right
Paul Rooney (2008).
'The Futurist' (production still), 26 minute video.

39 — Paul Rooney

In the Belly of the Architect

Iain Sinclair

We commissioned Iain Sinclair to journey through the SuperCity. First he travelled by car from Hull to Liverpool with filmmaker Chris Petit, then by bus-pass from Liverpool to Hull accompanied by wife Anna. The resulting reports, published here, form part of his first major work set outside the capital.

Photography Anna Sinclair.

I think, down here in the South, we got Hull badly wrong. It's something to do with the sound: Hell, Hole, Hull. Linguists call it 'goat-fronting', the innovations of young Humberside females; the way that vowels in words like 'goat' are articulated with an assertive thrust of the tongue pushing much further forward in the mouth than orthodox Yorkshire tradition demands. Young women, we discover, when we arrive at the once mighty fishing port, are confident, solidly built, active; token-dressing for a long weekend on the razzle with few concessions to climate, the unforgiving, in-off-the-North-Sea downpour. We've been misled by stereotypes customised for export: the crooked-mouthed, wife-beating old pro-cricketers, the saliva-spitting, would-you-credit-it pipe-suckers. And wearied too by John Prescott's mangled arias of self-justification and class war. (Conducted from state-owned, rent-free apartments and striped croquet lawns in the Home Counties.) Prescott has spent too long south of the M62. A colour snapshot complementing the inevitable punch-drunk shuffle into TV celebrity — an autobiography that reads as if it were dictated in a hospitality suite between promotional interviews — presents an alarming Dorian Gray portrait. Inside the flaccid sporran of superfluous, hard-dining flesh is the imprint of a rugged Heathcliff workingman, a union organiser who looks disturbingly like a fit and glowering Fred Trueman. A good metaphor for the way the North's ruined industrial heritage has been prostituted by grand projects of regeneration (new forms of colonial patronage).

My son recalled an ASBO family he knew, deemed too recidivist for Hackney, being expelled to the only place with a higher standing in the league table of crap towns: Hull. Which these unfortunates did indeed hear as 'Hell'. And took their leave, with downcast eyes and Dante-tread, as if walking barefoot up the Great North Road on a causeway of burning coals. Only to discover that Kingston-upon-Hull is reinvented, made-over, lavished with architectural plantings and The Deep, a flashy Terry Farrell dockside fish-tank with as much cultural clout as the Mayan-jukebox, M16 building on the Albert Embankment, on the south bank of the Thames. A drunk with a smashed nose was sheltering in a deep recess of Farrell's signature regeneration project when I visited Hull's marina at night. "I've fallen off me bike," he explained. Now bikeless and lacking coat or jacket.

Hull City — for a few hours — sat at the head of the Premier League, having spanked most of the high-spending, showboating metropolitan football franchises. Football is money, the sub-cultural Esperanto we all speak. Without much fuss or discussion in the broadsheets, Hull hoovered-up serious tranches of credit: development-fund malls, pedestrianised precincts, a TV screen on a triumphalist arch. Along with a decent railway station which featured a bookshop flogging a knockdown stack of Prescott's apologia. And, as the final stamp of media approval, a visitation from the architect Will Alsop in his high-wheel, off-road vehicle (with attendant film crew).

What Alsop was peddling, with vim and vigour, was his playful notion of a SuperCity, a strip development of doodle-inspired outcrops on either side of the M62, the Hull to Liverpool motorway. The TV projection is of a man who gives (and receives) very good lunch; excellent company, reflex smoker, statement-hair ruffled by the breeze, loose shirt, unstructured French-blue artisan's jacket. Freeflowing jazz monologues in a seductive deepthroat growl. Something after the fashion of the playwright Simon Gray: the smoker's smoker, the one who lights up to steady his nerves, while waiting for the oncologist's verdict. But with the heft and gravitas of Brian Dennehy in Peter Greenaway's film, *The Belly of an Architect*. Projects collapse, prizes are won, partnerships fold and are reformed. There is commissioned work in Germany and in France. And lottery-funded millennial crumbs in the English badlands, marginal constituencies unfortunate enough to be noticed by box-ticking central government. Rewarded, lunched, photographed. Then dropped like a child-molester once the latest renovation has been puffed and computer-enhanced for the brochure. A topography of virtual masterpieces that will never be built or operated. Architecture is the art of getting some other sucker to take the blame.

Discovered, nozzling his gas-guzzler on a northern forecourt, Will Alsop is an engaging presence who can't wait to grab his felt-tipped pens to riff on the windscreen. He fires a fresh cancer-stick and takes stock of his surroundings: "Cheap and nasty, horrid, revolting, evil, complete and utter shit." Here is a motorway utopian, an architect taking on enough work to free up the time for his true passion, painting. Painting on windscreens. As ludic conceits grow out of dim agribiz edge-lands, and storage boxes develop pop art warts and blisters, Alsop is revealed as an English version of the great Andalusian virtuoso in Henri-Georges Clouzot's documentary, *Le Mystère Picasso*. The one in which Pablo paints on sheets of glass, lightning-sketches in air. Coloured pens rattle across the dashboard. Contrails of tobacco afterburn. Thick gold signet ring on gesturing paw. An actor who can drive and talk at the same time, effortlessly. Man of the road. Service station philosopher.

Alsop strikes east out of Liverpool, making for that great enabler, the M62: for Hull and childhood memories. He schmoozes the camera, architecture as infotainment. "It's about playing," he says, gesturing towards a ravished horizon of cooling towers, no-purpose sheds and glinting rivers. "This is an itinerant area that you can't define as country or city." There is nothing quite so agreeable as pulling onto the hard shoulder, to tease a reef of Claes Oldenburg soft-sculptures out of innocent ground that would otherwise be polluted by Barratt estates: off-highway garages with dormitory provision. Post-nuclear family units resembling Travelodges broken down into their constituent parts. The film-maker Chris Petit, when we motored up and down the boulevards of Alsop's virtual city, admitted that, on the whole, he'd rather take up residence in a Portakabin alongside the smoking landfill mountain on Rainham Marshes.

It's a disposable form, the tactfully vandalised Alsop windscreen (with a little low-budget enhancement in the editing suite). What you get is an authentic dialogue between landscape (in cinemascope frame) and sketching, with its intimate, improvisatory charm. The problem, for me, starts when the cartoons slide off the rain-spotted window and into the planning process, the slick brochures of puffers and explainers, moneymen. There is nothing wrong with speculative architecture so long as it's not built. If your proposal is accepted, spike it. Try again, fail better. The M62 SuperCity is unimpeachable: as a concept, a provocation. Commission it and you deface its innocence, that tender membrane of novelty and risk.

Will Alsop is a figure for our time, the man on the move, a Travelodge-stopover businessman/artist with a story to tell. (Patrick Keiller, reprising Daniel Defoe's *Tour Through he Whole Island of Great Britain*, for his film *Robinson in Space*, spoke with great affection of the Travelodge franchise. You know exactly what you are going to get: strategic minimalism. Minimal efficiency, minimal fuss, minimal satisfaction. Expecting nothing, you are rarely disappointed. Anywhere is everywhere when you kip down, Crusoe-fashion, alongside a traffic island, within the soothing acoustic footprints of a peripheral, earth-banked motorway tunnel, designed to bypass outmoded concepts of a city centre. Which is to say: indifferent pubs, modestly crap restaurants, street markets

40 — In the Belly of the Architect

Photography Chris Petit.

peddling tat, charity shops and surveillance-approved crime. Dogs. People. Humans. The thrust is monolithic, following tributaries of investment, loose cash, towards the next Grand Project. A disposable future underwritten by sugar barons, alchemists of behaviour-altering additives, packagers of rendered meat: Coca-Cola, Cadbury, Big Mac.)

One of the salient features of the SuperCity is the off-road hotel, which Alsop presents as a catalogue of Chaucerian collisions. "People don't actually meet or talk in hotels," he told me, when I visited him at the offices of his architectural practice, near Battersea Park, in a leafy and salubrious riverside quarter of London. "If you go to a hotel chain, it's perfectly clean and comfortable, but the public spaces aren't there. You're not expected to sit around and mingle. They're missing a trick. All these guys, particularly travelling salesmen, have a lot of stories. Hotels are not creating the stage for things to happen."

<u>The M62 SuperCity is unimpeachable: as a concept, a provocation.</u>

In SuperCity, social interaction is important; partying, yarning at leisure over good food; the classic English exchange (in picaresque fiction) between travellers, pilgrims with experiences to share. Inspirational head-to-heads in a dimly lit bar from which all parties walk away unscathed. The one-night stands of reps, jobbing actors, evangelists, tribute bands, runaways, auditioning footballers, tourists, academics without tenure, used-book dealers, and petrol-company hatchetmen deciding where they can close another filling station.

Will Alsop, coming off-road, the shudder of traffic still in the vein, the hum of tyres on wet tarmac, has devoured the distance between discrete settlements — Burnley, Bradford, Pontefract — and decided that they are all the same. In a car, in the pod, you can cherrypick: a cheese counter here, a theatre forty miles to the south, parochial divisions no longer play. "If these people live in Barnsley," he told me, "and they want an upmarket shop, they go to Leeds. If they want a jolly good market — they used to have one of their own, but it's gone — they drive to Doncaster. If they feel like a good thrash in the evening, they think nothing of heading off to Manchester. They use this plethora of towns, cities and villages as one SuperCity. All I had to do was stretch the concept to take in Liverpool and Hull."

Framed in the window of his sturdy vehicle, Alsop as tour guide and prophet of centralism, is an icon. I mean the hieratic representation of a sacred personage, an image lasered into glass by the setting sun. Adrift on the M62, meditating on post-pedestrian England, Alsop is as much a representative of his period as Vincent Van Gogh in that blood-eyed self-portrait, *The Painter on the Road to Tarascon*. The Dutchman, an accidental tourist in the burning lands of the south, is compacted by the furious intensity of his mission; bent under the burden of instruments, fixed to a melting road. Alsop smokes, talks to himself (and his unseen audience), pushes on towards the next pit stop. A benign and cynical explorer penetrating a game reserve.

"If you take roughly twenty miles on either side of the M62, from coast to coast, there are roughly 15.4 million people. Your journey can take forever, because of the traffic or it can be clear and quick. That's how I came to the conclusion that it would be a very good thing to increase the density. All those towns and cities are charged with building more houses. What they do, all the housing providers like Wimpey and Barratt, they look at the cheap option — which is to build on the edge of existent centres. This is not good practice. There are lots of places in the middle of those cities where you can build. There is no shortage of derelict sites. There are vast tracts of car parks just waiting."

Liverpool remains a source of regret for the London architect, a spurned opportunity; a European 'City of Culture' lacking the bottle to push through risky, but potentially rewarding commissions. The offer, made to Alsop's practice and then withdrawn, was for the Fourth Grace, a contemporary embellishment for the Pierhead, to sit on equal terms alongside three 'iconic' structures: the Liver Building, the Cunard Building and the Port Authority Building. Will Alsop, chatting to the local spokesperson, the television writer/producer Phil Redmond, employs that degraded word: iconic. As does Redmond. It's a Tourette's syndrome reflex, when there is a whiff of regeneration loot, cultural carpet-bagging, in the air. Ordinary folk find themselves talking like PR brochures.

<u>Commission it and you deface its innocence, that tender membrane of novelty and risk.</u>

"We're looking for an iconic statement, a beacon statement," Redmond delivers, without shame. Which pretty much nails the problem: how to demonstrate expenditure, how to pull in the punters, how to get yourself written up in the shortest possible time. The Angel of the North paradigm. Solicit a high-concept architect with sat nav and a fistful of coloured pens and, before you know it, the foreshore will be invaded by a regiment of naked and rusting Antony Gormley multiples. Glitzy shopping malls and revamped marinas follow.

41 — In the Belly of the Architect

When Liverpool came to sell itself to the colour supplements — IT'S HAPPENING IN LIVERPOOL, EUROPEAN CITY OF CULTURE 2008 — it was with a sunset close-up of one of the naked Gormleys from Crosby beach; staring blind at the Mersey, the Corinthian portico of William Brown's mid-19th-Century Museum and Library, and a spread of anonymous twinkling towers. 'Diverse, energetic and exciting, it's a city that has something around every corner. Art sits in between stunning architecture, beaches lie half an hour beyond the bustle of chic boutiques and stunning new shops. Undeniably cool bars and eateries offer great nights out.'

"This is the western gateway," Will announces, slumped at the wheel, cruising once grand docks, tobacco warehouses converted into gated communities. "Nasty, horrid," he growls: demonstrating a genuine affection for the spirit of place. He's groping for a way to "celebrate uniqueness without changing the character of what is already here." The great thing, he acknowledges, as he rolls out of town, is that you can drive to Hull, by way of the M62, in less time than it takes to cross London. The obvious conclusion, as he sees it, is to make all this disconnected stuff, all these beacon destinations — Tate Liverpool, Ikea Warrington, Trafford Park, Libeskind's Imperial War Museum of the North, the Lowry Centre, Terry Farrell's The Deep — into one unified sprawl, an urban mega-development 20-miles deep. A fantasy island not unlike the grunge actuality of East London's A13, with its blue fence reservations, arsenic alps, rebranded Millennium Dome, Hawksmoor churches, oil refineries, retail parks, wind turbines, nature reserves, penal colony housing estates, landfill dumps, pylon forests, used-car forecourts, aspirational bungalows, MOD firing ranges, tolerated pockets of traveller-camped wilderness, pinball arcades and piers. You can't unpick such a cacophonous screech of competing human narratives, because there is always an underlying and resistant seam called: finance. Called: realism. One mayor hypes a future of new bridges, floating airports. The next one kills them.

"We won the competition in Liverpool," Alsop explained, "but it wasn't just architecture. There was a financial element as well. What happened was that there was another development, King's Dock. Their own development. It went over budget. They had to raid our £70,000,000. They weren't honest about it." The contract was cancelled. Leaving a regretful Alsop musing on betrayed visions, as he drove out of town. "The big asset they've got is the river. Fascinating streets with boarded-up pubs and wonderful sugar warehouses. If I was chief planner of Liverpool, I would be making this area as dense as possible. When you can look south over a majestic river, why do you build mediocre stuff inland, where you wouldn't want to be? It sounds very simple, but if you wake up to a good view, you feel better."

The dream highway of the M62 — undistinguished settlements at a safe distance, scabby moorland, the perpetual expectoration of cooling towers gobbing filth — summons reverie, recollections of childhood. Alsop grew up in Northampton. There is an affecting moment in his television documentary when he speaks about standing on a motorway bridge with his father, gazing in wonder at the traffic flow, road as river, before a family picnic in a neighbouring field: a final snapshot to treasure. His father died within a week of this excursion.

Hull, Alsop recalled, was the exotic destination for a holiday with a Northampton friend in the wet fish trade. "It was thriving, a real fishing port. On the other side of the river, they took all the elements of the catch, crushed at the bottom of the hold, and turned them into pet food. The whole of the edge of the port was full of women in pinnies gutting fish. All these people lived in terraced houses which backed on to the river." The workers, like the place itself, had a cherished independence. They were independent, not just of southern England, but of Yorkshire: of Bridlington to the north, and of the other side of the Humber too, Grimsby and Cleethorpes. I think of a son of Hull, son of a fishing-boat painter, Tom Courtenay: that ancient-when-young (and young-when-ancient) ship's figurehead smile. Carved whalebone, scrimshaw. The twinkling eyes of a recently decapitated cod. Actorly twitches flirt with an insolent disregard of approved and accepted metropolitan manners. He can't quite believe that he's got away with it for so long, this soft employment. No blood on the hands.

Alsop spoke of Mr Bogg, the employer on the docks. "'They're buggers,' this man said in affectionate exasperation. 'They steal all my wooden fish boxes to make furniture. I wouldn't mind, but whenever they have to go anywhere they ride in a taxi.'"

We saw those taxis. And the weekend-partying tribes of the Humberside diaspora, the granite banks converted into lap-dancing clubs. I arrived in May, early in the season, in Chris Petit's comfortable, diesel-devouring Mercedes, to check out Hull — and to launch our test drive down Alsop's SuperCity highway. When we stroll through the icy downpour that first evening, we are hustled by genial touts at the open doors of hard-drinking, red-light venues loud enough not to require further advertisement. The women are strong, comfortable, and dressed to please: to please themselves. A girl with a couple of bootlace-ribbons barely supporting a skimpy vest sits outside a pub, smoke-swallowing, chatting on her pink mobile, watching raindrops bounce off the round metal table. "You pregnant?" calls a passing lad. "Your breasts is standing right out, love." She doesn't bother to swat him away.

The town, with its generous civic spaces, close alleys, part-developed warehouses and docks, supports the Alsop thesis: collision, celebration, short-term local migration. A party town glorying in its Premier League status, its tsunami of new dosh. Helicopters shadowed us across over the Humber Bridge, as we cruised into a zone of imposing stadia, retail parks and pagoda restaurants. The clatter of blades dispersed melancholy flashbacks to suicide news reports, jumpers. I remembered Alison Davies, whose twelve-year-old son, Ryan, suffered from a hereditary condition called Fragile X Syndrome. Ms Davies travelled by train from Stockport: to plunge from the bridge with her son. The extended city is also a conduit for dark history, for disturbed and disadvantaged people at the end of their tether, driven to the limits of a particular and unforgiving geography.

There were reasons why I didn't visit Hull often enough to appreciate its now evident virtues. I was here last in the Eighties with a book-runner called Driffield. As we came over the bridge, Driff said, "Hackney can stop boasting about being the poorest borough in Britain. It's embarrassing to go into charity shops here. Women are fighting over secondhand knickers that are falling apart. You wouldn't see that on Kingsland Road. Hull makes our Oxfam look like Harrods."

Then there was the percussionist, pyromaniac and riverboat pilot, the late Paul Burwell. He got an art gig in Hull on the first wave of development money. He liked it, found an abandoned boathouse, and stayed: in what proved to be a tragic exile. A story I recovered, posthumously, from unreliable and highly-coloured reports. Burwell fell out with a community of travellers who shared his riverside wilderness. There were incidents, assaults. Beatings with iron bars. Returned from hospital, Paul took to his bed, keeping up his spirits, in every sense, with a diet of supermarket whisky, supplied, for a consideration, by one of the traveller kids. The lad turned a profit by cutting the whisky with antifreeze. Being of a strong constitution, used to running up ladders with knapsacks of petrol, Burwell lasted a few months on this toxic regime, before he was found: outside on the frozen earth, stiff as a board. That was the legend, the horror story.

The clincher, the ultimate deterrent, was Philip Larkin. While the bespectacled spider was in residence, I kept well away: as far as the Wash. For late modernists, Larkin was the antichrist; the sinister librarian with the schoolgirl bondage collection in the desk drawer. And a very canny way of managing a career by staying out of firing range of metropolitan fashion. Professor Eric Mottram, sponsor of adventurous internationalism, went white at the name of Larkin. He choked and spluttered in Herne Hill, denouncing Hull as an English Siberia. The university, now that we're up here, seems quite progressive, on the case. My enthusiasm might be coloured by finding more of my own books (actually stamped, read) in a local library than you'd excavate in fifty London Waterstone's outlets.

Firing ranges are relevant when you consider Hull's position on the map. In the autumn of 2008 the London Evening Standard reported that a Russian nuclear bomber had penetrated British defence systems by flying within ninety seconds of the coast. 'The Blackjack jet was allegedly carrying out a mock attack as it targeted Hull virtually undetected by RAF interceptors. The breach, thought to be the most serious since the Cold War has called into question Britain's defence capabilities. The supersonic jet had taken off from Engel's Air Base near Saratov on Russia's Volga delta.' News of Alsop's SuperCity had grown real wings.

Emerging from a traditional northern Tex-Mex diner, where portly middle-aged men feasted, swiftly and silently, with young women to whom they were not related, Chris Petit was handed a card for the Purple Door Club ('Nothing's A Secret Here: £10 per fully nude dance'). Too chilled by gusting vortices of frozen rain to contemplate a naked scamper, we ducked under the live television-screen arch — HULL UFO SOCIETY MEETING, DISCUSS STRANGE SIGHTINGS AND GHOSTLY GOINGS ON! — and skated like tumbleweed down the pedestrianised shopping precinct to our flag-bedecked hotel. Where I switched on the local news to have the identity of the trio of cultural heavyweights in the chopper that buzzed us on the Humber Bridge revealed: Bob Geldof (honorary knight of the realm), Elle Macpherson (acknowledged beauty, businesswoman, actor), George Foreman (ex-pug, preacher, non-fat burger griller). They had been airlifted to a covert assembly room to pitch ideas, to punch the envelope. This was no budget seminar. With another helicopter hop, a private plane out of Humberside International Airport, Bob and Elle were back in the Smoke for a charity black-tie bash the same evening. The Hull excursion as much a secret as a royal tour of duty in Afghanistan.

The following morning, raw from a sleepless night, Petit discovered that his silver Merc, secure in the hotel's basement garage, had been the scene of an unauthorised party. The night staff didn't waste the opportunity to entertain in a motor of that vintage and leathery comfort. After cleaning out the kebab wraps and knotted condoms, we headed for the M62. Stopping only to pay tribute to John Prescott's favourite trough, Mr Chu's China Palace riverside restaurant. A lion-decorated, green-and-red stockade that looked like the unstruck set for Nicholas Ray's epic, *55 Days At Peking*. Chuck Heston, gun-lobbying gladiator, was a wimp when set against the local Humberside heroes:

Prescott and Dean Windass, the shaven-headed anachronism whose goals propelled Hull into the Premier League (and a formal party at the hotel where we lodged). Finding an entire gallery at the unreconstructed whaling museum given over to football legends in striped shirts, I told Chris that I couldn't accept Will Alsop's contention, one of the articles of faith around which his SuperCity thesis was developed.

Step outside your car and everything changes. Wind bites. A road sign for Saddleworth has the Oldham part of it peeled like a second-degree burn, a failed graft.

"It suddenly struck me," Alsop said, "that if Leeds and their football team fell out of the FA cup, the natural thing would be for the supporters to cheer Manchester United or Manchester City. Then you have a regional identity, one city." About as natural, I thought, as incest. And much less popular. Leeds and Manchester United as companions in arms? Jack Charlton and 'our kid' sharing a damp Woodbine in the bath? Happy-go-lucky Billy Bremner tickling the ribs of Nobby Stiles? Trans-Pennine blood feuds are often a matter of two or three miles of disputed ground. If there is anything that unites the whole SuperCity, it's the quality of hatred: Liverpool-Manchester-Leeds. Badge-kissers, coin-throwers all.

The writer Michael Moorcock lived for a few years in a rambling house at Ingleton, close to the Yorkshire/Lancashire border. "No question that the Wars of the Roses lived on. The towns around Leeds all had very strong identities and a sense of superiority one to another. My friend Dave Britton says that although everything has changed on the surface in Manchester, with new council estates replacing terraces, the basic character remains the same. Markets where markets always were, violence where violence always was. The notion of supporting Leeds had him laughing like Bernard Manning."

The M62, Petit reckoned, along that first stretch out of Hull, was almost as good as East Germany; nothingness was absolute, our transit smooth, traffic light. The cooling stacks at Selby are always worth a photo or two. We pulled off-highway at Saddleworth Moor, to take in, from this rugged tump, the hazy spread of Manchester. Once again dark history oppressed us. You are never free of that back story, the abused and buried children. The ones who have never been recovered. And the malignant excursionists with their leaking newspaper faces: bottles of cheap wine, tartan rug and spade. The satanic version of Coronation Street.

Step outside your car and everything changes. Wind bites. A road sign for Saddleworth has the Oldham part of it peeled like a second-degree burn, a failed graft. Limestone giving way to Millstone Grit. A rough track leading to the Pennine Way. A microclimate of low cloud, clammy air you hesitate to breathe. Rubbish pits and tyre dumps in which unwanted things cook and seethe. Mesh fence protecting pylons barnacled with humming disks, eavesdropping equipment. Cars that stop here are suspect, furtive; out of place until the rubber rots from the wheels and they sink into the peat.

Coming the other way, east, as part of his television essay, Will Alsop pulled in for a comfort break. "What Saddleworth Moor needs," he said, "is more access roads and a fancy service station." He climbs out of his high chariot, yawns, stretches. "Let's make a beautiful rural service area at this point. With fantastic food and unbelievable shops." A 24-hour destination magnet appealing to the nightbirds of the SuperCity. Who would be? Entertainers, reps. Haunted solitaries. The feral underclass populating crime encyclopedias. Gloved wheelmen in white company vans cruising a connected network of red light districts. Tabloid monsters with claw-hammers and faulty moral wiring.

We looped Manchester, looped everywhere. When it works, and you float, nobody wants to come away from the road. We'd visited Liverpool a few months earlier, to shoot a piece for the Audi Channel, driving a £60,000 luxury model from the Antony Gormley beach into North Wales; so Petit suggested a detour to Morecambe. Which involved a Truckers' Stop at Carnforth that demonstrated all the qualities a moveable city should possess: space, light, colour, simple generic architecture with American windows. Comfortable chairs inside and a silent television screen pumping out Euro-junk football, with no drama, no hysterics. In the approved Alsop fashion, this refuge has no allegiance to the local. It was Belgium, Italy, Oregon. In a pleasure-seeking cartography of absence, cancelled villages and deleted histories, here at last was an oasis of the possible. It required no intervention from planners or icon-soliciting architects. Morecambe, half-revived, half-choked with the bad karma of the drowned cockle-pickers, was an unresolved argument between entropy and aspiration. With spectacular views and a sweep of bay for which the inhabitants seemed to have no particular relish. A woman, out early, dragging a blind German shepherd dog, chatted with a street cleaner in a yellow tabard. "He's moulting. It's fab. Like getting a new carpet for the front room."

Nothing we found, along the whole span of the road, had actually been built by Alsop. He explained, when I visited him in his office, that the idea of the SuperCity emerged over a period when he was involved with a group called Yorkshire Forward. "The man in charge gave me Barnsley. Nobody else wanted it. I was rather hoping to get Scarborough. The M62 became part of my life. If you go by train, it's hopeless."

The muddle of post-industrial towns expanded, in the exhausted driver's eyes, into one city; the best elements of entrenched settlements preserved, the worst destroyed. Then everybody piles into their cars for a weekend thrash in Manchester. The advantage of being trapped in Huddersfield or Goole, it now appeared, was that you could get out, fast, to find a better car park, a livelier Travelodge, a destination Ikea. "Manchester feels alright, once you're in. But it takes a long time. Nobody is quite sure where it starts or finishes."

I carried the book with me, the Will Alsop tribute compiled by Kenneth Powell. There was one surviving Alsop structure still to be located, the toilet block of the Earth Centre at Conisbrough, near Doncaster. It was from the era when New Labour was still a novelty and millennial slush funds, milked from lotteries and other addictions encouraged in those who could least afford them, were being channelled towards northern areas deemed fit for regeneration. (You have to be in Olympic trim to survive it.)

"A deal was done with the National Coal Board," Alsop explained, "to re-landscape the slagheaps. They actually had a vineyard. And a perfectly decent hut where you could get something to eat." A nice little project too successful to be left alone.

Then the terrible thing happened: they got the loot. "I remember when they rang me up, everybody was excited. They were going to give us fifty million. Unbelievable!" Fifty million expanded, as these things always do, to eighty. "Jennie Page was in charge of the Millennium Commission. You could see why she chose the Earth Centre: it was green, it was in the North. It was not in London."

A major public disaster was snatched from the jaws of a minor local success. "In retrospect, it was the worst news we could have had, the granting of lottery funds. The original group lost control. They were blamed for this failure, but it was not their fault. They never needed that huge amount of money. Our practice designed and built the millennium lavatory. That's my only millennium project."

Arriving in Conisbrough and finding no trace of the Earth Centre, we tried the Castle. The heritage custodians blazed and bridled: a sack of money down the drain, they reckoned. Nannying management (customers arriving by car were surcharged a fiver a head for wasting fossil fuel). The Centre lasted for two years, while it tried to work out its unique selling point. They finished up offering budget archery for kids. The story the castle-keepers told us was that Londoners came up, were given the best jobs and houses, milked the system: and jumped on the train as soon as the plug was pulled.

A melancholy Asian security guard, doomed to spend his days gazing at a surveillance monitor, and wandering slowly around the perimeter fence of what looked like an abandoned Guantánamo Bay, was delighted to have some company. Guard towers, a grass-roofed yurt, overgrown slagheaps. 'Combining futuristic architecture with poignant memorabilia from a mining past,' said the notice attached to a skeletal metal tree, an artwork. Here, at last, was a fitting monument to the SuperCity: a new wilderness ripe with the traces of a noble but ugly industrial past and the embryo forms of an abandoned future of computer-generated visions and bankrupt reality. Will Alsop, smoker, painter, driver, is our Daniel Boone, a pioneer opening up territory where we don't want to go. The SuperCity of the M62 is an installation that will never be achieved. A provocative television thesis delivered at a time when nobody is watching. A Grand Project outdated before it is launched.

Iain Sinclair's latest book is Hackney, That Rose-Red Empire: A Confidential Report, **published by Hamish Hamilton, 2009.**

Chris Petit's latest film is a 21st Century, post-crash road movie, provisionally entitled Economy, **for Channel 4 and Germany's ZDF.**

43 — In the Belly of the Architect

44 – Further

Further

Iain Sinclair

One warm June evening, coming away from the corrupted geometry of another generic docklands development, down a busy arterial road, Anna lost it: where am I? It was like emerging from a poppy-drenched siesta, not knowing if it were day or night, London or Blackpool. Was she a boarding-school pupil or a married woman? And to whose unfamiliar body, like a coat in the wrong size, was she returning? Our walk was endless, nothing connected with anything else; shifts in urban landscape were abrupt and meaningless. A pack of computer-generated postcards shuffled and spilled in any order; the soft pornography of regeneration challenged by minatory warehouses, film noir alleys and the sullen, sour-canal whiff of the real. Hard labour, speculation. We had travelled, on the diagonal across England, to achieve this: a fugue, a lurch out of time, the loss — for Anna — of present identity. The reconnection with an earlier child-self, a schoolgirl of this city: Liverpool. Spectres of memory do not fade. They wait, obediently, among the stones, on the gradient of an undistinguished street, to reassert overwhelming intimations of essence; the way we become what we actually are. Mortal, fallible, fated. But here, always here. Rewalking a lost place for the first time.

This was the necessary second chapter of the Will Alsop challenge: road-test the impossibility of the conceptual SuperCity. Having driven it with Chris Petit, stupidly, doggedly, mile after mile, I understood that we had adopted the idiot's approach. We rode through a geography that was never there. Nor meant to be. In the world of the Grand Project, the pitch is its own consequence. Any attempt to use a proposal as a working model is madness. It would be like taking Mervyn Peake's *Gormenghast* as the literal blueprint for a shopping mall in the Olympic parkland of Stratford. Or planting the golden pillars of a New Jerusalem, from William Blake's epic, in the cultural quarter at the back of King's Cross Station: a relocated gasholder. We must respect the primacy of the imagination. Alsop's strategic vision achieves purchase as a Second Life cartoon. Here, on the overspill of the M62, is the future we are burning up, the non-spaces we will learn to inhabit: the last humans, from a William Burroughs fiction, swimming into the coldest reaches of an infinite cosmos, equipped only with leaking aqualungs and an outdated Liverpool city plan.

From where we find ourselves, this June evening, displaced between Chinese wholesale warehouses, Hope Street bistro-bars, cathedrals and sanctified relics of Fernando Torres and Steven Gerrard, I hallucinate the siren song of the rusting naked figures on Crosby beach. Antony Gormley multiples drowning in the Irish Sea. 'The party of a lifetime.' Culture-bouncers are lining up to chuck us into the club: Gustav Klimt at Tate Liverpool, Pete Postlethwaite as King Lear. And thousands of sporting personalities, suited and shining, for another hysterical, premium-rate TV phone-in spectacular.

My idea was to trade on decrepitude, turning the stiff-spined, liver-spotted wasteland of a 65-year-old self to advantage, by riding across England, Mersey to Humber, on my Hackney Freedom Pass. It had been announced that the old ones with their orange plastic wallets could travel anywhere in the country on local buses: gratis. The hope being that numbers of newly privileged geriatrics would forget to come back, or take themselves off to edgeland asylums and terminal hospices (if they hadn't been converted into gated communities).

Anna joined me on this freedom ride through the back roads of Alsop's SuperCity; she had her own agenda, memories to set against whatever we would find. As, for example, the Adelphi Hotel in Liverpool, where we spent our first night. To Anna it represented the good place, that never-forgotten exeat in a time of austerity; afternoon tea served by white-cuffed waitresses in a high-ceilinged room as big as an opera house. The Adelphi, at the hub of the seatown's civic pride, was the secure and comfortable watering hole for businessmen, stopover celebs, expense-account politicians. Or so the channelled schoolgirl, her parasitical prior self, remembered: "A magnificent lounge with its acres of armchairs and potted palms, the elegant double-staircase curving away at the far end under the vast chandeliers and the mirrored glass." Everything except Gracie Fields, the Marx Brothers, Noël Coward and the ship's orchestra from the Titanic.

My own experience of the Adelphi was more recent. A very different movie: digital, collision-cut, sponsored. A paradigm of contemporary art practice: the hip advert disguised as yesterday's underground road meditation. The Audi Channel, who had squatters' rights somewhere on the outer reaches of the Sky satellite network, hired myself and Chris Petit to sit, for one day, in a £60,000 luxury motor bristling with cameras — and to drive from Crosby beach, through Liverpool docks and the Mersey Tunnel, out into the gloom of North Wales. We contemplated the threatened Gormley duplicates, admiring their stoicism, as wind whipped up a minor sandstorm and curs pissed against the slender rusted legs. Liverpool, seen through the frame of this absurdly solid, silent, purring car, was a sequence of random quotations, ordinary lives experienced and endured without reference to our predatory voyeurism. Petit asserted that England was now a discrimination of storage and distribution sheds: difficult to decide if we were looking at a Swedish furniture warehouse, a private hospital, an art gallery, a logistics operation or England's largest stack of soap powder. It took much of the day — soothing hum of tyres, steady rain, twilight border-country of secret bunkers and disused quarries — to dissolve and repair that single Adelphi night.

The train service from Euston was normal: that is, cancelled, glitch on the line at Milton Keynes, no further explanation or advice offered. A panicked mob charged, on a rumour, over to King's Cross. We stood, elbow to elbow, swaying, threatened by luggage, gasping for air, as far as Rugby. Or some other lost Midlands platform. The memory-system shuts down: the crawl on a suburban line around Manchester, before Lime Street and a latenight binge in a Chinese restaurant where quantity, lurid, toxic, fizzing on the tongue, attempted to make up for quality, for the racket of midweek celebrants. My room should have come with a complimentary bicycle. You felt like checking the light fittings for microphones, the wardrobe for families of Romanian gypsies. I was kipping down, soothed by a tinkling of broken glass in the street below, shouts, blows, in the theme park stateroom of a deposed regime: old Bucharest, the Moscow of Guy Burgess. Supersize furniture. Fire-sale thrones once used by Orson Welles as Cardinal Wolsey. A master bed fit for a stable of Aintree horses' heads.

But that was on the Audi Channel tab. With Anna, I got a modest cabin like a berth on the Dublin ferry. Eccentric and serviceable as anywhere else in provincial England: lacking the cigarette-scorched dog blanket and soiled vintage underwear (kicked under the bed), we had encountered, a few months earlier, in a hotel near Grafton Street in the Irish capital. It is breakfast that really sorts these places out: hot windowless basement, lukewarm food-substitutes scooped out of troughs, mud coffee. A complicated machine to incinerate slices of damp white bread. The new Adelphi, Britannia Adelphi (Liverpool), is the state-of-Britain film that Lindsay Anderson never quite got around to making; after rugby league in *Wakefield*, *Britannia Hospital* and *The White Bus*. Our breakfast bunker is packed with Arthur Lowe and Leonard Rossiter substitutes waiting for their coaches: Lakeland tours, Blackpool Illuminations. Ranked taxis offer to run three people (£45) or five people (£65), for three hours, on a Beatle circuit with 'lots of photo opportunities along the way'. Mathew Street, Penny Lane, Newcastle Road, Menlove Avenue, Forthlin Road, Arnold Grove, Madryn Street. Assorted blue plaques, tasteful memorial statuettes. The idolatry of exterminated Beatles is a major industry: bad boys, slick movers, sanctified by global capitalism and the local fetish for wakes and displays of public mourning.

Anna's Proustian lounge was off-limits, broken down into tables and booths, for a nutritional trade fair. If you are not badged and accredited as a healthy-eating vendor, challenged by the saturated reek of deep-fat eggs and irradiated bacon, you must be part of the theatre-going package: Anita Dobson in *Hello, Dolly!* Or the spooky Derek Acorah, medium and television personality, fronting a chat show with the loquacious dead. Acorah is a Southport man, ex-footballer, returned from the Hyatt Regency Hotel in Dubai and the Hotel Intercontinental at Al Ain. From time to time, he is possessed by an entity called Kreed Kafer (anagram: Derek Faker) With his wintry sea-wave hair and metallic eyes, he could step straight into the Second Life of a computer-generated panorama on the fence around a building site and be right at home.

Before we get That Bus, we are obliged to sample the Mersey end of the Alsop SuperCity: art, food, spectacle. The imperial heft, the Reich Chancellery weight ▶

Top
Photography Anna Sinclair.

Left
Photography Iain Sinclair.

45 — Further

and neo-classical gravitas, of that block of halls and museums, is impressive and a little intimidating. Anna's cataleptic episode on the dock road, her involuntary deprogramming, started with a high-speed art trek, the way we insult a city by cherrypicking its highlights in a couple of hours. I like the room of classical busts, old gods drained of blood, injected with formaldehyde, chilled into marble. Titular spirits who have seen it all. Shafts of pale afternoon light falling across city fathers, emblematic lovers. The Walker Art Gallery manages very well its heritage cargo of accidental plunder: Pre-Raphaelites trophy madonnas, competitive topography — and up-to-the-moment, city-of-culture commissions.

The picture of the month is a *Liverpool Cityscape* by Ben Johnson. An anamorphic spread, steely blues and airplane greys, so hyperreal that you know it's another computer-generated fiction, another visiting card from a future that will never arrive. Johnson, after working on a reconstruction of the Urbino panel, an ideal city attributed to Piero della Francesca, accepted a commission from Hong Kong Telecom to paint a panorama to mark the transfer of sovereignty to China. This *Liverpool Cityscape*, an angel's-eye view from high above the Mersey, stares unblinking at a planner's dream of a rational, regenerated, maritime city-state: with empty docks and the human element reduced to touristic dots on the edge of the cultural quarter. 'Some of the buildings,' the brochure admits, 'don't yet exist or are currently being built.' But the accuracy of their dimensions is unimpeachable: eleven studio assistants, consultations with historians, architects and planners, ensure it.

What need then of the old Liverpool, its narrow ways and loud cellars, its illegitimate legends, the failed speculations and faded department stores? The city is a museum of its own dissolution, dressed with freakish survivors: the golf-tee spike of the Post Office Tower growing out of a Holiday Inn, shop windows filled with OK! magazines duplicating the approved marriage portrait of Wayne Rooney and his bronzed and airbrushed bride, trompe l'oeil sculptures bursting out of severe buildings, superceded malls of budget tat and a major 'coming soon' development — GRAND CENTRAL — with ambitions to make Liverpool anywhere but where it is. Who is responsible for this plague of sponsored sheep, eyeless, hairless, plastered with faux graffiti: Morecambe, Crumpsall, Knotty Ash, Little Crosby? It all comes down, it climbs again: curved glass, brown brick, steps ascending into nothing, spindly municipal plantings. Beside the revamped docks, they have a car lot of silver pods plastered with stickers: NO INSURANCE SEIZED BY POLICE. Liverpool's famed surrealism, the way it lends itself to a poetry made from lists and brand names, remains active. Necrophile sentiment underwrites the heritage makeover: a glistening black Billy Fury, legs spread, gesturing at the cranes and grids of new white blocks. A chunk of bronze like a broken phallus alongside the open-mouthed vulva trumpet and some rusty rock. The reflex gesture of the immigrant group signalling the pathos of their conversion into a compensatory symbol. And then the spectacular red-gold gateway into China Town, Gilbert George Scott's Gothic Revival cathedral peeping over the top. Anna remembers, coming back to herself as we settle in an underground bar in Hope Street, being brought here by coach to take part in an anniversary service, to sing with the school choir.

The whole point of this bus gig was spontaneity. Anna had to restrain me from jumping on the first vehicle with free seats, pointing in approximately the right direction: kamikaze pensioners, rucksacked and black-bagged, half-smart (top half), we voyaged in expectation of the rising sun. A day of low cloud, dishcloth skies, mercury roads. Steady movement and, once aboard, no decisions to make: where you go, we go. End of the line. End of the story.

Liverpool buses, I do appreciate them. I stayed once, a terrace in the near-suburbs, with the poet Robert Sheppard. And the highlight was the ride, next morning, into town: the friendliness, the breathing space, the way this people-carrier manifested on demand. It was like being in Europe, in Dublin. Back home in Hackney, aggrieved clients step further and further into the traffic, to scan the horizon; willing the missing bus, any bus, challenging it, to make an appearance. For safety, these lumbering viral torpedoes travel in packs, stacked to the gills with munching, sneezing, multi-tongued communicators apologising for non-arrival, resetting assignations, critiquing dead television. Any stratagem to carry them away from where they are, this contemporary version of the prison hulk, the cholera ship. In Liverpool, travellers nod and chat, take in the scenery, discuss the reasons for their journey, cross themselves, and generally acknowledge the privilege of being chauffeured around town, in comfort, for a few coins.

Robert Sheppard, who had experienced it, full on, as rate-payer and citizen, composed a few words around Liverpool's status as City of Culture. 'Their shit's verdure but that's OK/ This isn't a nature poem.' Sheppard's near-twenty-year epic, *Complete Twentieth Century Blues,* outweighed the Ringo returns, the showbiz art: he cooked slow and long, with tangy sauces and bits that break your teeth. The city averted its eyes. No time or space for poetry in Alsopian relativity. The virtual, happening before it happens, spurns language that stops our headlong gallop, calling it a 'difficulty'. As if it were the poet's fault that we want our meat pre-chewed.

If the tongue's trail entered an entry without a thought,
Leaves no blood on a milky thigh, then there's
No story without telling, another
Day of congealed gloom.

We have a pack of timetables, but none of them make much sense. I'm impressed by the PR put out by St Helens (previously known to me as a successful Rugby League team, the Saints). A triumphalist player is featured on the cover of the Visitor Guide, showing off his Pilkington Activ TM sponsorship. That's the other thing in St Helens: glass. We have to get to this fortunate Eden on the borders of Liverpool and Manchester. The town has it all: 'spectacular sport, global heritage, culture and entertainment, drinking and nightlife'. A very Alsop-sympathetic attractor. 'One-time cradle of the industrial revolution... a growing regional destination of choice... with status as the most car-friendly place in Northwest England.' The whole pitch is flagged by 'a landmark new internationally significant artwork'. Which has yet to be announced. It will be unveiled later in year (subject to planning permission). It doesn't matter what this artwork is, or does, or who made it: until you have one, your Angel of St Helens, you are just another cash-soliciting carpark off the A580.[1] (A road number which looks to my soft-focus gaze very much like ASBO.)

If St Helens is the event horizon of our first ride, the immediate prospect, according to Merseytravel, is Huyton. There is so much room on the bus; in fact, the bus is a room, a waiting room in flight. Silver-grey tarmac speckled with mica, a river. Banks of red brick, baked mud: a high street running on forever. This ride is a powerfully transformative experience, molecules shaken up, memories invoked, how I travelled as a child between short-haul destinations in South Wales, towards markets or relatives: the cold, misted, greasy metal of the supporting poles, the backs of the seats, the coarseness of tobacco-infested cloth. Generous window panels break down the division between streetscape and fixed interior, we're clients of a single-decker with bright green poles and red request buttons. Old ladies are the only ones heading for Huyton, old ladies and their mild-mannered grandchildren. The ones who remind me of Welsh excursions in the company of women; mother, grandmother, great-aunts. I don't think, outside London, I was ever on a bus with my father.

As we pull away from the city centre, we notice how the threat of regeneration imposes a uniformity on cancelled terraces, the same blue shutters, old trade-names painted out. The long, uphill road is as unreal as the back projections outside the coach, as it escapes East Germany, in Hitchcock's *Torn Curtain*. Passengers accept their role as actors in this fiction, acknowledging our presence, but leaving it at that. This local bus service is the final democracy. Accents shift with the miles travelled, allegiances are a real thing: Will Alsop's elastic uniformity of interests doesn't play. Liverpool suburbs stretch but do not sprawl. A bus is not a coach (Freedom Pass holders pay for a coach ride). A coach is a train substitute. When Alsop was being processed through the North with the Urban Renaissance Panel and the other lottery fund commissars, a coach was sometimes laid on, never a bus. Luxuriously appointed coaches, with reclining seats and personal monitors, carry premier league millionaires from ground to ground: Wigan, Blackburn, Bolton. In the flat-cap, Woodbine-and-pint-at-half-time days, footballers took the bus. Coaches don't stop. They have tinted windows to ameliorate blight: to stop the curious looking in. Nobody looks out. They are electronically anæsthetised. The rare-bookdealer Rick Gekoski, when he wrote — in *Staying Up* — about a season with access to the players of Coventry City, found this to be the sticking point: would they let him on the coach? Not always, not with any great enthusiasm. Ginger-nut manager Gordon Strachan endured inquisitive outsiders with a poor grace, with gritted teeth and monosyllabic grunts. Gekoski demonstrated the metropolitan conceit, shared with Alsop: these clapped-out industrial relics are all the same.

'I didn't go to the next game, at Bolton. The reasons for this are obscure, even to me, and involve my prejudice against visiting northern towns beginning with 'B'. The idea of them depresses me, though I've never been to any of them, to Bolton or Barnsley or Bradford... Look at the names of those northern B-towns — Blackburn, Bury, Burnley, Blackpool, for God's sake — which sounded like places of interest on a tour of Hell.'

I kept Gekoski's paperback well out of sight. Anna grew up in Blackpool and went to school, between the ages of twelve and sixteen, slap on this bus route.

"Will you recognise Huyton?"

Would anyone recognise Huyton? Whatever ghosts it once possessed have been unhoused, the bus station is the best of it. A flatpack conservatory: polished glass panels, smooth yellow rails, Jagger-tongues of wilting green plant-life. We have an agenda here, to locate Anna's school, to validate that skein of the past, four seamless years, in which she was happy. The fissure in her life comes when she is removed at sixteen, sent off to another place, more bracing, academically challenging: a mistake. But a fortunate one for me, as our downward drifts carried us both across the Irish Sea to Dublin. There were a lot of buses in Dublin.

Crocodiles of schoolgirls parade the high street to the parish church: a half-remembered snapshot. Shopping expeditions on Saturday afternoons. Cabin-trunk at the station, the school gates on the other side of the road. Those things Anna recalled. The estate where the school once stood, pointed cliffs of red brick, reticent gravel driveways, they had been treated in the usual fashion: residential care homes, nurseries for 4-wheel-drive mothers, secure apartments. An awkward sense of badly disguised history to nudge your elbow. Voices from captured playing fields. Private roads dressed with weeds. Dogs barking at our approach.

"I should never have come," Anna said. Swimming pool, tennis courts, corridors loud with music. Brought back. Vividly present. "The chapel gleamed with flowers. There were groups of girls in the long cloaks we wore in the winter, hoods lined with the house colours."

Stalking the privileged enclave of this suburban development, we are the spectres the 1950's children saw; old ones who could not free themselves from a myth of the past. Our photographs are the confirmation: patterns in the bricks don't change, the chapel has the same narrow windows, trees are trees. We are divorced from everything we once were: those interminable Lancashire Sundays dreaming of escape.

My conviction that every bus station must have a decent café somewhere in the neighbourhood is proved wrong: McDonald's or nothing. The expedition I mount to humour my prejudice against uniformity rushes us through accidents of pay-off architecture, suspiciously well-funded libraries. Huyton is favoured by the legacy of its most celebrated MP, Harold Wilson (pipe in public, cigars and whisky in private). This is not one of those Californian vanity jobs, mausoleums of fixed history, shrines to Reagan or Nixon. The Harold Wilson Library is downbeat municipal and empty, shelves of Politics and Sociology for ambitious swots. But no maps of a place that is no longer there, nothing local in this locality. No copies of the booklet on Liverpool's Chinese community that I failed to pick up in the city.

Misreading a rumour on the internet, Anna tells me that Cherie Blair went to school in Huyton. When I re-enter the town in cyberspace, I find nothing but the news that Huyton College closed in 1993 and that the former school can now offer 'luxury mews housing, beautifully converted, within a secure gated community'. A connection is pointed out between Baroness Morgan ('former pupil of the highly selective, fee paying Huyton College') and Mrs Blair. Baroness Morgan of Huyton is fingered as Tony Blair's 'most trusted adviser'. She is unelected, a Tory. She 'wields enormous power... through the personal gift of Blair'. A fix is suggested, by which Morgan will arrange a safe seat for her close friend, Cherie. 'The Kirby Times expects an announcement soon.'

St Helen's has the first roadblock we encounter, the first detour: an undisclosed blue-tape incident. Concrete-slab police station with windows like mean nicks from a cutthroat razor. The low rail around the flat roof won't deter any convinced (or persuaded) jumper. A large woman in pink T-shirt, tight mid-calf leisure slacks, pink socks and trainers, is interrogating a white bag for that missing cigarette. Inuit-smooth, hunched, a no-neck ovoid, she seems built for water rather than the boundary wall of the police station car park.

We need a luggage rethink. My black bag is cumbersome. I choose a rucksack from a shop on the pedestrianised traffic island. The town refuses to live up to its PR boasts, it slumbers undisturbed around the statue of Queen Victoria, a promised comedy festival. "The spell of the journey is upon us," Anna says. And she's right. Local buses are addictive. Wigan sounds like a proper staging post.

The Scouse accent has flattened out, the patter. When you move as a passenger through unknown territory, there is no obligation to list particulars: let it drift. Metal-shuttered pubs and roadhouses with no road. Avenues of dwarf trees dress patches of worn grass. Our fellow passengers are tidy, lightweight sports-casual clothes and considered hair: they chat, some of them, turning a blind eye towards the themed George Orwell Wigan Pier pub, alongside the sanitised canal. An insinuation of pies and gravy, golden chips, makes Anna hungry. But we don't have time to stop, there's another switch to be made, another bus station.

A double-decker (MANCHESTER LIMITED STOP): upstairs, seats at the front. We're going to make it — and already there have been so many varieties of custom and behaviour; an inhibited retreat from the linguistic extravagance of Liverpool. Those Wigan pies sit heavy on the stomach, even when you see them stacked like geological specimens in a shop window. The bus crawls through miles of proud suburb. A gobby girl takes the seat to our left, chewing her mobile: "I'm not in a mood. It's you, right, you're in the mood. You're not listening: I'm not, not, not." A daily ritual, this affectionate abuse. Virtual courtship: phone-sex on a budget. She studies her nails. Places her feet, ankles crossed, on the window ledge. She alternates spite-riffs and lingering red-tongued licks at a sugar bag that looks like a plasma sachet. "You're trying to put me in a mood, you, so you don't have to see me tonight. You don't want to see me, I don't fucking care. I'm not in a mood, you're in a right mood. You are, you fucking are."

Garden plots nudge against this teenager's snappy solo, against trim estates: the complex gravity of Manchester's emerging blot. "Traa. Traa. Traa. Fuck off." She dismounts, leaving us alone; the bus in its descent, into the rain, is our personal limousine. A tour of brown-sign cultural highlights: Trafford Park, Salford University, the Coronation Street Experience. High-angle perspectives down terraces that are still terraces and aspirational cul-de-sacs with broad grassy pavements. Tudorbethan multiples with apron-lawns, hedges and shrubs and stuttering cars from driving schools with self-important logos.

I've never made any impression on Manchester. There isn't room for two cities in my life and it's too late to start now. Even as an itinerant bookdealer, I worked my way around the edges: Huddersfield, Halifax, Hebden Bridge, Todmorden, Rochdale. The rain is unremitting, we need to find a place to stay that is convenient for the bus station. The nest I select, over other Travelodges and future renovations, has a pitch: licit, centre-city, in-transit sex. In the best possible taste. With boutique dining. 'Be more rock 'n' roll next time you visit... Indulge in one of our suites, loaded with the latest gadgetry, dressed top to toe in the slinkiest of interiors. Enjoy power showers for sharing and tubs in front of the telly... Interiors with real balls and fire... A doll walks in... well, the place was once a doll hospital, someone fix her up.'

Very Rio Ferdinand. Very Caligula. The posthumous wet dream of Bob Guccione. Straight to video. Do-it-yourself Polanski. But a very decent night's kingsize, crashout slumber after the shuddering of the buses, the hungry road. A segment of canal outside the double-glazed window, the ink of industrial heritage.

Next morning, a uniformed doorman with a branded umbrella chases us into bar-code rain.

"Car or train, sir?"

"Bus. In the general direction of Hull."

Anna pauses to admire a scrawny young woman stilting over the crossing towards Piccadilly Gardens. A little cropped jacket. Bare white midriff. Sky-high black heels. Fishnet tights and tiny denim shorts, wide leather belt decorated with metal studs. Thin blonde hair scraped back in a ponytail. And pushing a baby buggy, with attitude, on her way to ram-raid Mothercare. While giving the infant a good rinsing. Weaving among fountains, as liquid-shrapnel bounces from the paving slabs. "I love her style, her energy," Anna says. "Two fingers to the weather."

A Manchester bus, single-decker, for the climb towards Oldham's ridge; wipers going like a North Sea trawler. Cranes loom over unfinished, and probably abandoned, concrete skeletons. Chinese distribution centres. Converted Methodist chapels. Our craft heaves and pitches: junk yards, botched scams, a townscape with which I am very comfortable.

Sitting on one of the back-to-the-window (seen it all) seats, at the front of the bus, is an old fellow whose portrait I have to record. A Lancashire music-hall turn, all nose, collapsed cheeks, mouth like a ring-pull. He mumbles, rehearsing his patter, a litany of grievances. A stoic comedian who has run out of straight men. Ratty suede jacket with fake astrakhan collar, rain sodden. Nose dripping steadily. A stalactite mime of melancholy and malfate who makes me feel glad to be alive.

Opposite him, and unaware of his presence, are two young ladies of this city, beauty reps, old hand and novice, one white, one Asian: in flow, alive, with accents to charm us with their vivacity and rhythm. (Unlike Coronation Street. That soup of Scouse, Geordie, Brummie, Salford. A collision of jobbing actors, club singers, fruit-fly celebrities. With, from time to time, a cracking script.) The girls are dragging their demo equipment around with them, folding tables, bulky black bags. The newcomer, the round-faced Indian girl, never stops talking, so that her companion, checking with her supervisor on the mobile, has to shout: disconnected overlapping dialogue. They love their work and wear it, painted masks of small perfection. They are industrially perfumed too: against the urban mold of sodden gaberdine, the consumptive hacking of the drowned bus. The hooped spines of demi-cripples transported through a catalogue of tall chimneys and dark canals to their proper Lowry setting. A rattle-bag of museum-quality relics glorying in their redundancy.

At the Oldham terminal, we pass out of one timetable, through a building that reminds me of Athens airport and the ever-shifting and reconvening queues for various island destinations, into another: the connection for Huddersfield. Nobody can convince me that the cultural shifts we are registering — weight of pies, speed of speech, attitude to surroundings — could be brought within a single system. Or that such a system would be desirable. Huddersfield passengers have an upland quality about them. Braced for the Pennine transit and delighted to be riding, not marching off, heads down, into the mist.

Chip shops. Chinese restaurants. Hairdressers. A slow ascent with many stops to take on students who immerse themselves in their books and iPods. Getting away from Oldham involves another detour around a blue-tape incident, blood on the stones. After Saddleworth, a heritaged watermill, Yorkshire announces its difference. Anna admires the labour that has gone into rows of immaculate and competitive gardens. Over damp moors, the view from the front of the bus is romance: grey and green with soft hills in the distance. Farms and scattered villages.

A change of driver and, after all these hours, what Anna describes as "a party atmosphere". Like refugee families returning home after the Blitz. A young woman, loaded with bags, climbs out of the bus, miles from anywhere, the nearest farm barely in sight.

Food. I haven't allowed the time for such indulgences, it's out of one bus and straight on to the next. I'm not convinced, although I don't admit it, that we'll find a way to make that ultimate connection, back down the M62 to Hull. In Huddersfield a woman at the information desk suggests Pontefract. For a start we should try Wakefield. Provisioned with bus-station pork pie (an ice-hockey puck welded out of doggy chews), with flapjacks and scalding coffee, we're on the move again. Difficult to sip and suck in this trembling vehicle. Up North, buses are not cafeterias in the London style. The odd schoolkid deflating a crisp packet or puncturing a can of fizz, that's all. We dine with extreme discretion, hunkered down in our seats. I hop off at the first halt to dispose of the half-drunk carton, the crumbly evidence.

We pass a field of scarlet poppies. "Isn't that a beautiful sight?" a woman remarks, as I take the obvious photograph. "The farmer must have made a mistake."

Wakefield, with its low-register colours, is no longer the town of Lindsay Anderson's *This Sporting Life:* homo-erotic propaganda, psychodramas of physical hurt and otherness. Richard Harris, fists bunched in donkey jacket, makes the social ascent from bus to showy Jag. Grudging envy to uncomfortable local fame. Stay on the bus, lad, that's the message. Stick with your own.

Old film is a memory flash as we rush for the Pontefract connection. But it's not Pontefract anymore, it's a retail and transport hub known as Freeport. Without intention, or prior knowledge, we have arrived at an outpost of Will Alsop's SuperCity. It's off-highway, grown out of nowhere. All-purpose, non-specific warehouses: restaurants, white goods, fun palaces. Anonymous hotels double-glazed against the roaring river of motorway traffic. A consumerist oasis built from a doodle on Alsop's windscreen. He's not the architect, Freeport is post-architectural, self-propagating; he's just the prophet.

"The road is the only absolute."

Bus stops in Freeport are covered stands of the sort you'll find in the long-stay car park at Stansted. There is one connection for Hull, miss it and we are done for the night. Anxiety is palpable, the requirement to be in the right place at the right time. Rain falls remorselessly. Buses for other destinations come and go. Our stand is shared with two old ladies who have heard the rumour of a possible Hull transfer, a bus coming down from Leeds, but they can't confirm it. A young couple, bored and hormonal, feast like fast-food addicts. The girl hungrier than the boy. She burrows under his sweater, nipping, biting. Swapping wads of gum, mouth to mouth. Meanwhile, he drains a bottle of Vimto, before drumming with the empty, kicking it against the glass. Then opening another in a sugary spray. They grapple, pinch, slap bellies. My linen trousers, I notice, are black with the road, oily dirt from picking up bags left on the floor of the bus. All my clothes are wet. I run across to the NEXT discount hangar and re-outfit myself for £7. The old ladies are cheerful, a great day out. "We've been to Frankie & Benny's, we've had us diners."

Leisure, commerce, strategic planting, easy access to road and rail: Freeport is the proof of SuperCity, everybody has an unconvincing reason to come here, nobody has much motivation to stay. You could dismantle any part of it without loss. The XSCAPE block promises cinemas, restaurants, shops, bowling alleys and an indoor ski slope. When you escape history, this is what you get. Freeport is where all the leftover topographies come together: seaside arcades, off-highway truck stops, suburban-rim warehouses. Storage, distribution and self-service have combined to form a computer-generated lagoon of non-space. A direct assault on the last remnants of the local. The canal system is now an opportunity for leisure-heritage, Orwell-themed pubs, boutique hotels, city marinas. The road is the only absolute. The condition of the airport — consumerist paranoia, expensive parking, unreadable architecture, terrorist alerts, celebrity visitations — is the universal model for the new England. Language as the final casualty. FREEPORT isn't a port and it certainly isn't free. Newspeak: 'Freedom is Slavery, Ignorance is Strength.'

Forty-five minutes late, our bus arrives. The young lovers were running out of permutations of engagement: her soft-cannibal assaults, nipple-tweaking, hair-tugging, and his Vimto-sucking, Vimto-drumming, narcissist indifference. Darkness was closing in. We reconnected with Alsop's super-highway, the M62 to Hull.

The Magical Mystery Tour. The White Bus. The Electric Kool-Aid Acid Test. Ken Kesey, Ken Babbs and Neal Cassady: further. It's an enduring fantasy. "Are you on the bus?" (Much less enduring when Kesey brought the restored wreck of the psychedelic freedom-bus to England for a pathologically dim and sick-spirited run to the West: what begins as vision ends as a funny-hat circus, a freak show sponsored by television. Arguments over plane tickets, wrestling matches in the mud of Blackheath with the promoter. You can't go back. You can't sample the same madness twice. Stick with the prescription, granddad. Stay on the farm.)

All the passengers, sea-facing now, across the shadowed land, are women; tawny, fluffed-owl hair, used-gold with a little red. It's like being in a compartment of office cleaners, on the wrong side of dawn: solidarity, anticipated exhaustion. The sights — Selby's belching cooling towers (steam from the mouth of a megaphone), bridges, motorways on stilts — are too familiar to notice, though we feast on them, rattled and stiff from two days of travel, hauling bags on and off buses.

This broad highway induces reverie. We are booked into the same Hull hotel I visited with Petit and I look forward, very much, to a free day exploring the town, before we take the train back to London. But I know that this road, the M62, has its victims.

A S HAULAGE, HULL LIMITED. Blue trucks like a school of dolphins accompany us to harbour. Drivers are secure in their pods, high above tarmac. The soft English landscape is a film that watches you: nothing to be done. These men are exhausted, bored, but aroused by the pulse of the engine, the steady vibration of movement. The gentle eros of night, the unknown. Road myths of pick-ups, casual encounters. B-movie existentialism.

MULTI CAR PILE UP. 'A lorry driver who caused a multi car pile up on the M62 last year was sentenced to four years in jail and a six year driving ban at the Hull Court today. One of the cars involved in the incident on October 19, 2007 was being driven by 36-year-old Jayne Shaw and her nephew, 17-year-old Stephen Parkhouse who had just started his second year of a four year joinery course at college, was a passenger. Both died as a result of the collision.'

Old newspapers, blowing in the wind, tell the same tale.

'Lorry driver whose vehicle overturned onto a car on a motorway, killing a driver, has walked free from court. Ms Taylor, 63, died after the 39-tonne lorry overturned onto her car at the end of the M62. The lorry driver was acquitted despite evidence from the Department of Transport's code of safe practice which proved that the lorry was too heavy. Mr Kynaston said that he did not know that his consignment of scrap fridges and cars was an unsafe load.'

You can set the beast at cruise control (this other driver did), American speed, mid-fifties: burger, cigarette, porn stash. Trousers around ankles. Masturbating as he ploughed into the stationary vehicle. Death headlines. Road-reverie shattered. You can break the dream. A man called John Davies walked the road. 'I spent the whole of September and October 2007 walking the motorway corridor, Hull back to Liverpool. This blog records my daily diary and reflections on the experience. The journey over, I'm resting my feet... I'm hoping that the break will give me some time to start to process this experience of walking... Thanks to the Liverpool Diocese Department of Lifelong Learning.'

The Hull bus terminal is right alongside the railway station. "Done!" Anna says. With justified emphasis. But the journey is just beginning, the first flickers of a new addiction: random excursions on local buses, the Freedom Pass to Freeport. We've achieved enough to have one morning on the town, no report to be made. Back to the Old Whyte Hart for a plate of the best fish, chips, mushy peas in England: the ancient pub where I stood in the rain with Petit. The contrast between the original whaling museum and the content-less Terry Farrell 'icon' on the dock. Having ridden all those miles, we have to acknowledge that a marina is a marina, Liverpool or Hull, different oceans, same artworks. The family-group sculpture from Albert Dock on the Mersey has arrived before us. It's another multiple. In Liverpool they are emigrants, in Hull they are immigrants. Sentimental paperweights between sea and M62, idealised pilgrims walking blind through after-images of the SuperCity.

A few months later, down on the south coast, I picked up a child's book from the 1950's, called *By Coach to the Seaside*. A post-war fantasy of well-behaved but wildly enthusiastic suburbanites and their marine excursion. "I thought we were going to the railway station, when, best of all it turned out to be the motor-coach station. Isn't it a lovely big motor, Babs?"

The countryside, they view it with a delirious excitement (and absolute suppression of detail). They ignore the comics bought for the journey. 'There were far more thrilling things to see outside.' Including a blockade. 'Once, they had a real thrill because the coach was held up by a policeman.' Who diverted them down a narrow country lane. Which led to that magical place, the seaside: recently recovered from its floating mines, barbed wire and commandeered hotels.

The bus driver, a white man in a white coat, has a parting word to offer.

"Be sure and have a good holiday, won't you?"

"Rather!" chorused the two.

And they did.

---

[1] *Now revealed as Catalan artist Jaume Plensa's 20m high, 400 tonne artwork, Dream. It is errected on the site of the Sutton Manor Colliery and was commissioned by a group of former miners. This white stretched head of a sleeping girl is visible from the M62 motorway. (Ed)*

Fail Better:
The art of Paul Bradley

Dan McClean

On the eve of his latest venture, Let them eat cake, a collaborative pâtisserie project that includes 'A Daily Bread' — a collaboration with Italian artist Michelangelo Pistoletto (whose first production graces the front cover of this magazine) — Yorkshire art maverick and veteran Orgreave protestor Paul Bradley talks with The Trials of Art author Daniel McClean about conceptual art in Halifax, visionary monks, bin bags and, of course, cake.

True North. Paul Bradley (1988). Dean Clough. Polished stainless steel. 1400 x 300x30mm. Image courtesy Paul Bradley & Susan Crowe.

Paul Bradley is a creator who has lived multiples lives. He has been an actor, performance artist, political activist, artist, and developed architectural and design practices. I first met Paul in 1993, as a producer of artists' projects at the Henry Moore Sculpture Studio, Dean Clough, Halifax.

Paul, along with Robert Hopper (former director of the Henry Moore Sculpture Trust 1988-1999) and Sir Ernest Hall (the owner of Dean Clough) was instrumental in creating the Studio. This consisted of two huge, beautiful spaces located in a 19th Century, former industrial mill (modelled on Renaissance palatial architecture) in Dean Clough, Halifax. The Studio was an artists' projects space and, above all, a place for artists' dreams and ideas. It was run by artists, under the guidance of Paul.

During the early 1990's, the Studio developed experimental projects with many leading international artists (particularly of the 1960's and 1970's), including Lawrence Weiner, Giuseppe Penone, Ulrich Ruckriem, Jannis Kounellis, Richard Long, Bruce McLean, Christian Boltanski and James Turrell. The Studio created a unique context for producing and showing art — a context that was neither a gallery, nor a museum and that had the intimacy and laboratory-like feel of the artist's studio. It is hard to overstate the importance of the Studio as a model of artistic production both in England and internationally, at this time.

Paul, who managed the artists and the Studio, is a pivotal figure in the arts of the Transpennine region. Operating over decades, and driving forward key projects, he has been a behind-the-scenes force in breaking new ground for artists and audiences. Without his direction, courage and understanding of the art world many influential projects would not have taken shape here. He is an unsung prime moving maverick of the SuperCity, who continues to inspire with his energy for radical, innovative artwork.

Part 1: Dean Clough

Paul, I would like to you to begin by telling me a bit about how the studio at Dean Clough came about.

What can I say about Dean Clough? Well, it was based on a number of wonderful chance meetings. However, chance meetings only take place when those involved have prepared for them by virtue of their attitude, intellect and practice. I went there in 1986 wearing a pair of raggy-assed trousers, living on income support from the State, which was amusingly entitled Enterprise Allowance, and I happened to meet a most engaging individual who was able to combine the talents of being both a classically trained pianist with being a multi-millionaire. This was Sir Ernest Hall, a very important person in my development. While the locals of Halifax were slightly suspicious of his intentions, he talked to those who would listen about creating a new working and cultural environment where art, commerce and innovation would develop together. He liked my attitude and gave my colleagues and I the top floor of a mill where I devised the installation and performance, *The Humdrum Plan*, a work derived from the repetitiveness and monotony of working life.

One day, in 1988, Robert Hopper visited my studio at Dean Clough. I already knew Robert, who was the founding Director of the Henry Moore Sculpture Trust, through presenting my work at his former museum in Bradford. We discussed his idea of how to create an artists' Project Room in the proposed Henry Moore Institute in Leeds. The properties that he was looking at in Leeds were proving to be restrictive, and as I was about to move into a new space I suggested he take my studio for this venture. Robert became inspired by the possibilities of Dean Clough.

The other key people were Sir Alan Bowness, chairman of the Henry Moore Foundation, who supported the possibility of a production/exhibition space for contemporary art, and Barry Barker, then at the Arnolfini Gallery. Barry had invited me to exhibit at the Arnolfini, and during the run-up to the project I met him and Giuseppe Penone, who was exhibiting there. Barry was keen for Penone's project to be seen elsewhere in the UK, but there were no takers. With the support of Dean Clough and the Henry Moore Foundation, Penone's project became a trial run for the Studio in 1989, with the Foundation extending their support for him to make a new work. Following Penone's project we closed the space for a few months and restored it to become the wonderful space you remember. No architects were involved, I just worked alongside the builders.

Can you talk a bit about its other elements, such as funding, and the links with industry to create the works and the artists involved in the Studio?

The financial aspect is important. One of the main reasons why great projects were created is that the Henry Moore Foundation, through the Studio, developed the backing to support artists in the development of their work. The funding was in place, we did not need to fund raise, and we could concentrate on the production process and creativity. We could be ambitious, and the projects could border on success or failure. The Studio was a laboratory. However, we were not funded excessively, just to the level of a regional art gallery's exhibition budget. We were canny in the production process. As artists, we had connections with industries in the region and could get good prices.

We were also lucky. We were dealing with a wave of creativity that was present within contemporary art at that time and dealt with major artists who were at important stages in their practice. Yet you have to have balls about this kind of approach to producing art. We went out and got these artists. We used to have to pinch ourselves as we sat eating bacon teacakes with Kounellis or Weiner in the workers' café at Dean Clough.

Who selected the artists?

Robert and myself. We discussed developing international artistic practice. We also discussed the rhythm of the space. How one expression would follow another. The steel and cast iron of Jannis Kounellis was followed with the more delicate materials of Wolfgang Laib. We were expecting Laib to work with one of his major materials, the pollen he collected from bees. Instead, he wanted to make his largest beeswax chamber, a process that consisted of casting 3m x 1m slabs of beeswax, in a round-the-clock production, as we could not allow the beeswax boiler that we had produced to solidify, as it took so long to melt the wax before casting.

Perhaps we were creating an essay in artist's practice or the life of a space. The real programming of this space was based on this rhythm.

There were art spaces at this time in Europe like the Hallen für Neue Kunst, Schaffhausen, Switzerland, and the Magasin, Grenoble, France. Both of these spaces were created in industrial sites that had been given over to contemporary art. Schaffhausen was also a former textile factory like Dean Clough and had established an important collection of work of artists from the 1960's and 1970's (many of whom worked at the Studio). However, Schaffhausen was more like a museum with its own collection. The Magasin was also an exhibition space. The Studio extended the model into artistic production.

Schaffhausen was dealing with the notion of exhibiting elements of a collection over very long periods so that due consideration could be given to them. Magasin was in the main an exhibition space dealing with large installations, some aspects of which were created for the space. We identified with what certain artists were doing with their own practice and spaces. In these new artist spaces in Frankfurt, Clonegal, Garessio or Marfa, artists were virtually curating their own work. So when we offered them a space, funding and support to make a new work, it fitted with their practice. Many of them were carrying ambitious projects that the experience and connectivity of the support staff at Dean Clough could realise.

The Studio was primarily a space for artists, and that conditioned all our activities. Artists recognised this and they proposed works that they had thought about but not necessarily found the support system to produce. A good example of this is Turrell's 'Ganzfeld Sphere'. Turrell's art deals with perception. As a young man he was a student of perceptual psychology and interested in NASA's experiments to prepare the astronauts for the moon landings. Part of this work involved Ganzfeld, or 'entire field' experiments, that centred on testing individuals in extra-sensory perception through introducing them to new sensory inputs. Part of this work involved submerging the head into chambers with coloured lights. As an artist, Turrell later produced smaller spheres that you could put your head in, or telephone booth-sized forms to sit in, but now he wanted to create a four-metre diameter sphere to take the entire body lying down. He was looking for a place to achieve this, and the Studio was that place. He created a huge Ganzfeld chamber, which he called *The Gasworks*, where the participant was laid down onto a bed and then rolled into the chamber, a bit like a MRI scanner. You spent fifteen minutes in the chamber and experienced an established sensory programme created from neon and strobe lights. This programme had to be passed by a perceptual psychologist from Oxford University in order for us to open the project to the public. Turrell and ourselves chose to lighten the preliminaries to the experience by having the operators dress as medical staff, and we prepared a waiting room with magazines for them. For the publicity we sent appointment cards to the great and good of the art world.

So this really advanced his practice?

Yes, and we were really pushing the boundaries so that Turrell could achieve 'grey light' without inducing epilepsy.

There were many important visitors to the Studio in the first years. Hans Ulrich Obrist, the leading international art curator, now curator at the Serpentine, London, came a few days after it opened, and Sir Nicholas Serota, director of the Tate, was another early visitor.

Everyone associated with the production process at Dean Clough was an artist who gave up time to create a special system for innovative projects. Whomever we worked with, be it Kounellis, or Weiner or Turrell, these young artists threw themselves into the projects. The eventual works, while undoubtedly being key works for these major contemporary artists, were very much a collective process.

Do you think this said something particular about the North of England?

Certainly, it's a socialist process. The process of Northern working people. We dealt with major artists. However, they were democratic about the studio process. They took care of us, and we took care of them. While the eventual work was undoubtedly theirs, the means of production and the terms on which that production took place was collective.

Do you think that there is something utopian about this?

Totally. Ernest Hall referred to Dean Clough as a 'practical utopia'. He came from an impoverished background in Bolton, but music saved him, and he obtained a scholarship to Cheethams, the music school in Manchester. When he bought Dean Clough, some of the locals believed he would simply asset-strip it and demolish the mills to sell off the stone. Well, it was quite the opposite, he developed the arts, innovation and commerce there. He built on that stone.

So this post-industrial utopianism was a significant factor, and this was soon after a period of industrial unrest and dispute, and at a time of recession?

Yeah, the miners' strike was still fresh in my mind, particularly my experiences at Orgreave.

Do you think the model of Dean Clough had to inevitably end?

The model should have ended after the first nine projects. Three-to-four years of activity. It really went on a little too long. However, we became involved in other projects, such as the Henry Moore Institute, and off-site projects in the region that developed into Art Transpennine. The Studio came to a natural end with the unfortunate passing away of Robert Hopper in 1999.

Part 2: The North

You have a strong political, emotional and intellectual connection with the 'North'. Can you talk about your experiences here, and how they have influenced your development as an artist?

Throughout the late 1970's and through to the late 80's Manchester was a musical oasis. But many of these young musicians were very serious and cultured people. Ian Curtis, for instance, was an extremely well read individual.

In the mid-to late-Seventies there were phenomenal bookshops in Manchester, some of them run by Michael Butterworth, the publisher of Corridor8, and David Britton. Both ran, and still do run, the publishing company Savoy Books, Michael's

50 — Fail Better

other publishing company. When they started out they opened bookshops across the North West, in Liverpool, Leeds and Preston. Ian was a frequent visitor to their Manchester shops. He shared a love of William Burroughs with the publisher, and dropped references to Kafka and Ballard in his lyrics. We (Stuka) were also serious and well read. We were also arrogant. At theatre school my performance art group was called Stuka, from the myth of the Beuys plane crash during the Second World War in Russia, when Beuys was apparently saved by being wrapped in furs and animal fat. Our first performance was entitled, *We Are Very Knowing Bastards.*

But how did you get access to this information? How were these cultural texts disseminated?

I just told you, we were very knowing bastards! We read. Science fiction was very big, but so were the modern and contemporary classics. Everyone was reading Burroughs. We were also into Céline, Morse Peckham, Theodore Roszak and Beckett. Roszak's *Where the Wasteland Ends* and *The Making of a Counter Culture* were important. The 'poor theatre' of Jerzy Grotowski, and Tadeusz Kantor's *Dead Class* were also important. I went to Berlin to train with Grotowski's actors in 1981, and later I brought them to the UK to train my theatre group and students. And back in Manchester there was a real vibe, and important characters such as Tony Wilson...

So Manchester was an important factor.

Sure, but not just Manchester, the whole of the North. Remember, from a social and political perspective we experienced the punk revolution, the "Winter of Discontent" and the Miners' Strike here. Key events and experiences that shaped attitudes. I recall being at Orgreave in a line of miners and supporters, arms linked, with the police a metre away from us tooled-up in their riot gear. Then a rumour spread that some old guy had recognised his son in the police ranks almost opposite him. Some families were divided then, but what made this striking was the fact that his son was not a policeman, but a serving soldier! It beggars belief. I believe Tony Benn refers to this in his Diaries. Then the police horses came and all hell broke loose. After, there was an eerie calm. I could not believe what had happened, and I have a difficult perception of the police to this day. Needless to say, I didn't bother to film it.

So that raises an interesting question. Do you think that there are certain aspects of political commitment and belief that cannot be expressed in art?

Perhaps, but the link I want to make is more of a socio-political observation, in that the Miners' Strike was arguably the last possible opportunity for the working people of this country to claim access to what was rightfully theirs — their participation in the profits derived from their labours. Now, although Arthur Scargill, the miners' leader, may have made some mistakes at this time, the greatest mistake was the inability of the working classes, and more specifically their executives, to mount a national strike. Hardly anyone else came out. They, and the East Midlands pits, were driven by fear and insecurity. If there had been a national strike then imagine the effect on our social, political and cultural destiny? Would it have been as significant as the 1968 movement, which brought both political and cultural change? In Europe, many artists, particularly of the Arte Povera movement, were politically active in '68. Kounellis and Penone from this movement showed at Dean Clough. In the United States, some of our major contemporary artists were assisting kids to dodge the draft.

In socio-cultural terms the punk 'movement' was important, and a great working-class music and fashion experience. Girls made dresses out of bin bags, and we dressed from and for the gutter. You made fashion from other people's throw-outs. This is very important when reflecting on today's Primark, credit-dependent culture. Then, you had to work to get originality; today you have to search for it.

What is happening now in the North?

These are different times. There are signs, and they are very encouraging. The Manchester International Festival is taking a quite interesting position and is relatively experimental for this type of organisation and event.

Last year a real public artwork took place. Following the tragic death of the legendary Tony Wilson, his friends and colleagues considered a memorial event or monument for him. Most other cities would have erected a statue or some form of memorial. But Manchester knew that a statue could never be conceived because the bugger was always on the move! What they decided was to hold an event that looked forward and did not look back, and one that embodied the cultural entrepreneurship of the man. They invited people under the age of twenty-five engaged in cultural activities to send in their ideas for a project, or something they wanted to realise. They then invited a large number of these people to a 24-hour workshop where the friends of Wilson and those associated with his activities spent time with these kids and gave them guidance of how to take their ideas forward.

This is a great commemoration to Tony Wilson — a kind of anti monument.

I would like you to talk about some of the other projects you produced. I remember two in particular that I thought were outstanding. One was with James Lee Byars at The Temple of Four Winds at Castle Howard, and the other was the series of exhibitions of Dom Hans van der Laan. Could you describe how you created these projects?

I had met Byars in Germany when I was at my gallery in Koln. Byars had phoned ahead to see who was there, and he was told that a young English artist was visiting. They also told him that I had recently become a father. He turned up an hour later dressed in a black velvet suit, the trousers of which were turned into his boots — 16-hole patent red Doctor Martens. He wore a tall red velvet hat, and his blindfold had slipped around his neck like a huge cravat, on top of which was a thick red hangman's noose. In his arms was a jeroboam of champagne. He complimented me on my dress (Yohji Yamamoto), held out the bottle and said, "Here's your baby." It was a good meeting.

A few years later, when he was invited to create a work for the Fondation Cartier, in Paris, he proposed a 3.5 metre diameter gold sphere set on a gold pedestal. The sphere would also contain a poet who would quietly recite poetry during the hours of exhibition. The work was entitled The Monument to Language.

When I went to see him in Santa Fe we talked about the Temple of Four Winds at Castle Howard. James and I had visited there a few years earlier. He shared my interest in follies as being places for reading and thought. Indeed, we are talking now in a small wooden estate hut, that acts as a folly. James and I discussed the relationship between the Four Winds, four philosophers, and the aspects of philosophical attitudes in the North, South, East and West. We decided to invite four philosophers with 'northern', 'southern', 'eastern' and 'western' philosophical perspectives and we would give them a question to respond to. I remember asking James, "What's the question?", to which he responded, "What is Question?" So the four philosophers met in the Temple on March 8th, 1996, in front of an audience, and stood outside their respective doors and delivered their response. Neither James nor myself were present at the event. He was fighting for his life and I was present at the birth of my second son. I received another baby and James survived for a few more years.

And Dom van der Laan?

Here was a monk, an architect, a theoretician who spent over twenty years researching his practice before he built. He only built four buildings, three monasteries and a private house. Incredibly, because he found the mathematical ratio, 'the golden section', too limiting, he devised, as a young man, his own system of measurement and proportion, 'the plastic number'. Later in his life, through the analysis of sites such as Stonehenge and, believe it or not, the Scottish Tartan, he realised that the plastic number was not something he had invented, but rediscovered, something that had been lost to humankind. A perfect conclusion for a Benedictine monk.

As you know my own practice had become more associated with architectural space as opposed to the art object. I was taken by how proportion and volume could condition human experience and the perception of a given space, and I had begun PhD by practice research on this subject. This resulted in four exhibitions, three conferences, three publications on van der Laan and the foundation of the Van der Laan Stichtung. I was helped by Richard Padovan, the leading expert on van der Laan.

How did you discover him?

Rudi Fuchs suggested I visit a monastery at Vaals on the Dutch-German border. So the non-believer, the virtual pagan, paid a visit. I remain a non-believer, but I began to believe in van der Laan's architecture. The experience of entering the atrium at Vaals was incredibly special, and this was only superseded by seeing the open cloister to the rear of the monastery. Here was volume and proportion developing and conditioning experience. For me it was true experiential and perceptual space.

As for the four-year project that followed this visit, well it is too much to go into detail in the time we have. I could write a book about it, a conceptual art detective story.

What do you mean?

Well, the abbot and the monks were always very welcoming, and after our first meeting they told me they could trust me. However, they only gave so much during each visit and they would almost tease me as I left. They would show me early models, drawings and teaching aids, then, as I left they would smile and say "When you come back we will show you Stonehenge." I would drive away from Vaals buzzing, and wondering what the fuck they were talking about. When I returned a few months later, there was Stonehenge — a perfect scale model of the complete structure cut and polished in granite and a portfolio of eighty or so drawings measuring and analysing the structure. Van der Laan had sent a team of young monks to Wiltshire and had the whole site surveyed and measured.

I like the sense of how you go from Byars to van der Laan, practices that are so very different on the surface, but they are unified by thought. This is a very important component in your system of producing projects.

Process is the aim, product is a consequence. Van der Laan's research and teaching aids may appear as wonderful conceptual art objects, but they are simply the products of a thought process and an aid to communicate this process.

Left
Gasworks: A Ganzfeld Sphere. James Turrell. (1993). Dean Clough. Image courtesy Paul Bradley & Susan Crowe. A 3.5m diameter fibreglass sphere with a white interior containing neon and strobe lighting linked to a programmer.

Top
The Red Cloud. Paul Bradley. Haags Gemeentemuseum & Rochdale Canal, UK. (1994-95). Image courtesy Paul Bradley & Susan Crowe. Red emergency blankets, canal boat and horse. In Manchester this formed part of the opening to the exhibition Duck not on a pond, curated by Daniel McClean.

I am delighted that, after many years away from art, you are returning with a very interesting new project. You are linking art, design and gastronomy in let them eat cake. Can you tell me something about the project?

The missing ingredients from your list are social interaction and human responsibility. Patisserie is a culinary art form, and this project combines artists and designers with innovative pastry chefs. From an artistic point of view, the cake could exist as a sculptural form; or it may form a plinth or iced white cube with a key object on the top. The surface of the cake may also be the basis for patterning, text or elements of painting.

However, for once the art element is not the sole issue. The issue is the social interaction of the public experiencing and consuming these items, and the responsibility of the project is to use as much of the income as possible to aid World Hunger, particularly with their work in the Democratic Republic of Congo and Afghanistan.

This is linking art with social practice.

Yes, it's a social, cultural and political project. One that has strong correspondences with the *Love Difference* programme of Michelangelo Pistoletto and the people of the Cittadellarte in Biella. The project involves an interesting adjunct to an artist's or designer's process, and a new correspondence with the public, but for once my more serious intentions lie elsewhere.

Let them eat cake, so that they may save others.

Are there any other projects under development?

In terms of architecture, a new domestic ecological residence in an orchard in Puglia. In terms of art and memory, I am also involved in a project to give James Lee Byars the Venetian exhibition he deserves.

You are very interested in eccentricity and you consider this to be a redeeming cultural value. How do you look on the eccentric? Do you see it as just an aristocratic virtue?

No. Eccentricity is a condition of attitude, not class. Vivienne Westwood for example, and if I remember correctly, is the daughter of a cobbler and mill girl. For me eccentricity exists where people with ideas and attitudes do not fit into a given socio-cultural system. I have a lot of time for eccentrics. I have considerable respect for Vivienne Westwood for her design, her attitude and her ideas. For me she is more of a thinker than an eccentric. Society terms her an eccentric because of her ideas and attitude.

I prefer the quiet eccentricity of the pure creative process, devoid of influence and market economics, just following a daily practice of thought and activity.

Is that why you have established so many different practices? You have moved through these positions, these processes. How do you see that? Some may see that as a fractured relationship. Or the process of a flâneur.

It's process, simply a process. The defining of a creative process that may start in an extremely expressive art form, 'poor theatre', then distil to performance and installation, then just to the art object, then just to the space containing that object, then just the space. A contraction in a way. Probably influenced by one of my cultural heroes, Samuel Beckett, whose process of expression contracted in both word and the body of those speaking. From a tramp, to someone in a bin or buried in a mound of sand, to just the mouth of *Not I*.

So where did that contraction begin, and where is it leading?

Well, I mentioned the poor theatre of Grotowski. This was a process where artifice was stripped from the performance, with the expressive capability of the actor's body and voice taken to new levels. Very intensive physical and vocal training, with feet bleeding and voices singing like hallucinating angels. The aim was to strip away the artifice of the actor to reveal true expression. A little like how Penone chipped away at the wooden beam to discover the tree inside. Poor theatre and poor art.

I have worked to maintain that chipping away, the removal of artifice, the minimalist or rationalist expression, the qualities of all that is poor; less can be more if you are able to achieve it on your own terms.

Is that something that we have lost in contemporary culture and art?

Yes. We do not understand the joy of having very little, just the essentials. In terms of the art I made, in 1994 I was offered a huge space in Essen to make a project. Ulrich Rückriem had used it in the *Documenta* exhibition in Kassel. This space was set in a former colliery, which was being turned into a cultural and educational site. The space was over 100m long, twenty-five metres or more wide and very high. What could I do, but turn the space in on itself. I installed eight huge loudspeakers in the roof structure, and they virtually disappeared. On a tape loop I then read out the names of all the UK collieries that had been closed down by the British government since the Miners' Strike. The work was called *Where Words Fail*, and perhaps that was my Orgreave moment.

I remember going to Glasgow some time ago to see Lawrence Wiener's films, and a colleague told me that Lawrence was looking for me and he was kind of pissed off that I had stopped making art. When we met up we talked things over and he remarked that nothing had really changed, other than the form I chose to express myself in.

One of the things you are talking about is a conceptual purity.

Yes, but the trouble with the art of our time is that the majority of artists make the same thing day in day out, and they do not really expand or risk their creative process. I make a distinction between artists who deal with form and those who are termed conceptual. The duty and privilege of an artist is to work, take risks, defy dreams and define their process into new and changing forms. Beckett puts it much better:

"Ever tried. Ever failed. No matter. Try Again. Fail again. Fail better."[1]

This is what artists have to do. Not the casual process of success, but the exacting process of failure.

This is an inscription of the humility in genius.

Exactly.

Daniel McClean is an independent art producer and art lawyer.

[1] *Worstward Ho. (1983).*

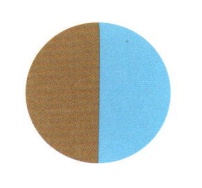

Standing in the way of control: Superflex, tenantspin and Alan Dunn. An investigation into social media

Marie-Anne McQuay

> "In 1999, as part of an experimental internet TV station called Superchannel, Danish art collective Superflex initiated tenantspin for residents of a Liverpool tower block. The project was conceived to empower local communities to produce their own web-based television content."

Bold Street Project. Filmmakers Chris Bernard and Alex Cox dressed as priests. (2007).

The project was intended to enable residents living in Coronation Court, Liverpool's oldest high-rise dwelling, to have a means of making themselves heard in plans to redevelop Liverpool's social housing. Demolition was being proposed for their homes, to be replaced by low-rise build. The residents objected strongly and, by taking part in *tenantspin*, were able to focus their efforts to de-rail the process. Contrary to prevailing beliefs they made it clear they preferred the tower block to other housing systems, provided it was properly maintained. Under the influence of social artist Alan Dunn, and to help raise the profile of the channel, celebrities, renowned writers, artists, musicians and designers were invited to collaborate with the tenants and to take part in programmes. These included the author Will Self, the KLF's Bill Drummond, Auto-Destructive Art founder and political activist Gustav Metzger and the playwright Jeff Young — currently in the press for his adaptation of Pete Townsend's *Quadrophenia* for the stage — who imagined the destroyed tower blocks rebuilt as a futuristic Tower of Babel.

There is no doubt that the project has had an effect beyond its remit. Since its origins in Copenhagen, Superflex went on to establish nearly forty such Superchannels around the world, in the United States, Thailand, Morocco, the United Arab Emirates and beyond, before it was retired by the artists in a group e-mail sent to all worldwide participants on 3rd December, 2007.

Yet the maverick tenantspin, the first outside Superflex's home ground, is still going strong after ten years of activity, offering a potent creative challenge to individuals and to any disenfranchised community.

The channel has a potential to empower tenants throughout the Alsop Super-City. Could it give voice to a widespread desire to live in high-rise — a prospect central to Alsop's vision of freeing-up congested city centres, reducing sprawl and creating leisure space? New Superchannels could be established anywhere there is a need for social empowerment, enabling residents to take control of their environment.

Marie-Anne McQuay's investigation into the tenantspin project asks the question: can socially situated art actually be effective? In doing this, she looks back to the ideas of 1960's UK art collective the Artist Placement Group, their relationship to Joseph Beuys — and at how best to keep alive a practice that sets out to affect institutional systems.

Flexing muscle

Danish art group Superflex developed their radical internet-based Superchannel project in a period that saw extremes of both optimism and pessimism around new technology: in the late 1990's the global economy was still artificially inflated by the illusory dot.com boom, whilst unfounded fears about the impact of the Millennium Bug were yet to be fully allayed. The rapid expansion of the internet's decentralised communication systems that the project harnessed occurred in parrallel to the rapid expansion of urban redevelopment in the North of England: the base of one the channel's longest running hubs. From an unlikely intersection between a technologically charged international art project and the UK regeneration industry came the remarkable citizen-led project tenantspin.

tenantspin was first commissioned through the media arts agency FACT (Foundation for Art & Creative Technology) at their Video Positive festival, and is developed and produced by social housing residents in partnership with FACT and a registered social landlord, Arena Housing. The starting point for Superflex's project was to provide the tenants of Coronation Court with a platform to raise concerns and seek to exert some influence over the threat of upheaval brought about by demolition proposals, part of the regeneration of social housing in Liverpool during the late 1990's. In addition, it provided all involved with an opportunity to test out the potential of an emergent technology — the internet — as a medium for citizen-based transmissions that ran counter to the centralised control of television and radio broadcasting.

Can such politically charged, socially situated, art projects really intervene productively in social contexts? Do they merely act out representations of social interaction, aestheticising rather than empowering communities? My article explores the wider questions that emerge from the story of *tenantspin*, from the aspirations that motivated its founders to the later direction initiated by artist Alan Dunn who steered the project from 2001-7.

Agendas and idealism

Since the pilot project began in 1999, there have been conflicts of interest over what a community-driven channel could and should do. These areas of tension highlight the differing levels of influence held by *tenantspin*'s many stakeholders, in particular the influence held by those who funded the project. Whilst most art invokes patronage to some extent, whether public or private, the patronage of a state funded housing association comes with its own agendas; in this case, a reluctance to alter the course of plans already set in place. Consequently, during the project's history, there have been clashes between this overly prescribed funding and commissioning scenario, and the practice of artists who seek to challenge established systems as an integral part of the collaborative process.

Superflex, a collective formed by Bjørnstjerne Reuter Christiansen, Jakob Fenger and Rasmus Nielsen in 1993, carries out a contemporary form of 'social sculpture', a term coined by (political) activist artist Joseph Beuys to describe art works that intervene in social systems, moulding the stuff of everyday life rather than conventional sculptural materials. Their interventions occur through art works or 'tools', which are created to be used independently by others, outside of art world contexts. Whilst their strap-line, "All humans are potential entrepreneurs", echoes Beuys's well known quotation, "Every human being is an artist", their choice of the word 'entrepreneur' over 'artist' indicates a crucial difference. They are pragmatists, as much as they are idealists, explicitly adopting the techniques of global capitalism to roll out their projects in the here and now, rather than seeking an alternative world in an indefinable future. Their proposal for a tenant-led, internet TV channel in Liverpool occurred through a convergence of trends in politically engaged international art practice and regeneration-led public art commissioning in the UK, with Superflex offering a service that would suit the agendas of all involved.

Coronation Court, the original site of what was to become the *tenantspin* channel, was one of more than sixty high-rise tower blocks whose management had passed in 1993 to a new government body charged with regenerating social housing in Liverpool: Liverpool Housing Action Trust (LHAT). LHAT was one of six other temporary national Housing Action Trusts set up by the Conservative government to run for a twelve-year period, with the tenants ultimately choosing a new permanent housing association landlord (Arena Housing) to manage their homes after this period. Whilst taking control of social housing away from local authority was politically divisive and indicative of wider schism between central government and Labour controlled councils, such a move was welcomed locally by the majority of tenants who were frustrated by the decades of neglect and subsequent deterioration of their tower blocks.

At the end of the 1990's the residents were facing an uncertain future with LHAT, namely the prospect of being re-housed. It should be noted that whilst the tower blocks were in poor condition, high-rise living was not itself unpopular, contrary to the negative national public image of the tower block ▶

as a failed utopian project. Most tenants had lived together for decades and were proud to be the earliest pioneers of high-rise living in Liverpool; they had developed a real sense of community in their 'streets in the sky'. Consequently they preferred plans that were based around renovation, rather than proposals for new low-rise housing which would potentially disperse them across sites and which many saw as a step backwards towards the terraced houses from which the majority had been moved in the 1960's.

Meanwhile, Liverpool arts institution FACT was preparing the new media festival Video Positive 2000. Many of the festival's art works were produced through FACT's Collaboration Programme, whose mission it was to affirm the organisation's commitment to new media art in participatory art commissions with specific communities. FACT had long been interested in the work of Superflex, and seized the opportunity to bring them into partnership with LHAT. The hope was that the project would be mutually beneficial to both parties: Superflex was looking for the opportunity to try out its new venture, Superchannel; Liverpool HAT, on the other hand, was keen to develop a public arts policy that would encourage community participation during this time of transition and avoid commissioning, in the words of Community Development Manager Paul Kelly, "an endless stream of murals and half-hearted community arts projects involving work of dubious merit and little local ownership." In addition to Kelly's enthusiasm for innovation, the bringing together of an ageing population (the majority of tenants were then aged between fifty and ninety) with new technology was a strategic venture for LHAT as the project fitted in with a wider government drive to deliver public services electronically and bridge the 'digital divide'.

Thus it was, through the mingling of artistic and social agendas, that Superflex were invited to recruit a group of tenants from Coronation Court and help them set up a dedicated web TV station for the block. Initially, bringing the tenants who volunteered to take part together with new technology, was a challenge in itself, since most had never been on-line before, and therefore needed to be introduced to the potential uses of the internet before launching into producing their own programming. Subjects began to emerge: father and son team, Jimmy and John Jones, created a weekly sports programme; Elaine O'Hare and others presented themselves as oral history subjects; Olga Bayley, one of the project's most passionate champions, urged other tenants to use the channel as a part of a campaign to save the block; Superflex themselves took their cameras to a HAT board meeting where redevelopment plans were discussed, making the officials accountable for the first time to a wider public. Other key programmes with lobbying intent from this period include webcast interviews with the original architect of Coronation Court, Rex Brown, then aged in his eighties, and Dutch architects Biq Architecten who had won a European award with their proposal to refurbish Coronation Court but who were still no closer to being commissioned.

The broadcasts were a high profile feature of the Video Positive Festival, gathering regional, national and international publicity around the tower block, whereas previously the issue of redevelopment versus demolition had been very much a localised issue even within Liverpool itself. Yet despite the project's profile, the activity it generated still did not force a decision in the resident's favour, and development plans remained stalled after the six-month pilot had run its course. Although Superflex originally stated that Superchannel would present the residents of Coronation Court with "a set of new media tools... to influence decision-making processes about their future" , their influence in reality was always destined to be limited by the agendas of the government-sponsored agency that funded the project. Whilst the art world may be regarded as one of the last refuges of left-wing utopian discourse, it is not without its own constricting obligations to funders and state bodies that affect in turn how much intervention is possible. Whilst artists may consult with communities as part of collaborative commissions, such feedback will be ignored if it does not match the objectives of the project's patrons.

When writers such as Barbara Steiner describe Superflex's practice as "radical democracy" they are investing a lot of faith in processes which highlight social inequalities but stop short of the real choice that a 'radical democracy' presupposes. However, if the project lacked the autonomy necessary to effect change in the short term, Superflex did more than stage symbolic debates within the art world; most of the labour of the project took place outside of the art world in the form of real rather than æstheticised interactions between the residents and their housing officers and the residents and a wider global audience which had started to engage with their programmes. As well as providing a new social setting for the tenants to engage with each other, it could also be said that Superflex's activist agendas changed how some of the tenants viewed themselves, from people to whom policy was done, to potential agents of change with access to a public sphere beyond their immediate local context.

Superflex's commitment to handing over the tools of production, the channel itself, after the six month pilot, rather than defining this as the end to the project, set up the possibility of a series of interactions that could span months and years, rather than the more conventional days and weeks of most art commissions. This in turn allowed the tenants to self-determine a use for the channel over time as a platform for debate that, through its sustained profile and diverse audiences now exerts greater influence over its funders than was possible in the early days when it was more of a niche art world project. This was, in many ways, the most 'radical' aspect of this project, the harnessing of a new technology that enabled local concerns to reach a worldwide audience.

Technological commitment

As facilitator of user-generated content, Superchannel pre-dated mainstream video hosting platform YouTube by six years, and had a more radical intent. Whilst YouTube's pithy slogan "Broadcast Yourself" exhorts the global visibility of individuals as an end in itself, Superchannel's comparable mission statement, "Make sure that you are seen and heard in the 21st century", was a call to the citizen to participate in the internet as a new public realm. Yet how did this technological idealism manifest in a pre-broadband era?

Originally, Superflex intended for the Coronation Court channel to become the communications model for "every tower block in the city", so that each high-rise would have its own webcasting studio. Superflex's aspirations bring to mind the image of illuminated tower blocks, beacons transmitting to the world in a physical manifestation of the decentralised nature of the internet. The channel had also been designed with the innovative capacity for live interactivity, enabling an on-line audience to join in the webcast and interrupt proceedings by posing questions in real time.

The political implications of decentralised distribution and the potentiality of interruption were very important to a project which sought to enable a form of peer-to-peer communication, in direct opposition to the centralised and passive communications model of television. The project was innovative, therefore, not just because it took place before webcam culture turned the sharing of everyday life with strangers into a social norm, but because of its total commitment to active participation in this new digital realm.

Its innovations also meant that people needed to be convinced that the effort needed to engage with the project were worth it. The relatively complicated technology needed to be heavily facilitated, as did the generation of content,

54 — Standing in the way of control

and after the success in terms of attracting participants in one block, LHAT agreed to provide funding for a channel that would be open to residents from all LHAT sites, rather than just Coronation Court. FACT, seeing the potential to test out a process-led, technologically focused artwork, then appointed a new project manager in artist Alan Dunn.

Dunn was a graduate of the Environmental Art Department at Glasgow School of Art, an influential cross-disciplinary course founded in 1985 that encouraged its students, who include Simon Starling and Douglas Gordon, to make work out of the "context of the world, with or through people." Dunn, reflecting back, states that, "We were asked to find our own relationships with different social situations, and I took this to understand that as 'social artists' we needn't always be in the centre of it all... it seemed important to me to step back from situations and quietly observe." Dunn therefore spent ten years working in the 'field', with the world outside the gallery as his primary context, commissioning billboard projects that interrupted the flow of consumerism with æsthetic interventions, alongside other public-realm works, and working within community projects that had the sharing of authorship at their heart.

Shortly after he took over, however, the whole purpose of the project seemed in jeopardy when it was announced that Coronation Court had been scheduled for demolition rather than redevelopment. The idea that the channel could have any influence during this period swiftly became redundant since decisions were ultimately to be made centrally on a cost basis. Activist artistic agendas lost out to a state body with pragmatic intentions, namely to efficiently replace problematic high-rise buildings with easy-to-maintain low-rise developments. Therefore, despite the support of local LHAT Community Development Officers who shared the resident's belief that redevelopment over demolition was the best course of action to maintain a community, what happened to Coronation Court became a pattern which ultimately left only twelve out of the original sixty-seven blocks standing by the time the HAT sites were handed over to new landlords in 2005.

Rehabilitating the Modernist social housing project with 21st Century technology was suddenly one more unrealised ideal, and the idea of the public actually influencing the course of regeneration seemed dead in the water. However, the *tenantspin* channel remained. Centralised in one studio, rather than embedded across the low-rise developments that were to follow, the tenants and the project endured and thrived. For the project to maintain and grow after the Video Positive Festival and to continue to produce content that was also compelling enough to attract a regular audience, some of the ideals of decentralisation had to be abandoned and production become more centralised. Alan Dunn quickly found, therefore, that the model of analogue television provided many solutions to a potentially alienating platform.

Thus a core team were trained-up like a TV crew to iron out technical glitches, and the tenants who programmed content met regularly so that webcasts could be researched rather than improvised. Webcasts were scheduled on a regular basis with a programme listing sent out by e-mail so that audiences knew when they could watch a programme live or catch up with it via the archive. To create an atmosphere, audiences were bused-in like a TV chat show. Content was collaboratively made but distributed through this one on-line channel, rather than independently by individuals, in order to maintain quality of output and maximise audiences.

Even so, Dunn was aware that only a small proportion of tenants would ever be convinced to watch *tenantspin* on the clunky PCs situated in the community flat. Innovative experiments were put in place with digital signals and CCTV systems so that programmes could be picked up on a terrestrial television channel. Although transmitting locally rather than globally, these programmes crucially allowed people to watch in the comfort of their living room. Dunn also created projects within *tenantspin* that were based on communality rather than technology, producing CD projects with tenants contributing songs alongside established musicians such as electro-band Ladytron in addition to other projects that could first be encountered outside the context of the internet. These included a party that was also a live performance by art collective Foreign Investment, which was primarily for tenants but also filmed and later webcast, and a series of audio commissions by Chris Watson, former member of Cabaret Voltaire, that were embedded in a tower block and featured on BBC Radio 3 before being transmitted.

Reflecting back, Dunn knew that some of these alternative approaches came too late and that *tenantspin* was destined to remain for the period of his involvement a niche project within a wider context, involving twenty to thirty tenants working intensely at any one time but incapable of embedding itself in a decentralised form. He knew that a community radio station or cable TV channel would have involved a wider group of tenants in production and yet, he also acknowledges that Superchannel was important for what it represented and how that affected what was produced: there is a difference in how one mediates oneself when the world may potentially be watching. The possibility that the project therefore was held to be both seen and heard on the world stage made it different from more traditional community arts projects that often reinforce marginal identities at a local level. Technology has also now caught up the project, with the widespread advent of broadband and wireless networks, and *tenantspin* is now also fully integrated with mainstream social networking platforms; whilst this in many ways makes the project less 'alternative', such mergings have allowed *tenantspin* to gather an even wider regional, national and international following whilst maintaining its singular socially engaged focus.

Art during a housing crisis

The demolition of Coronation Court starkly revealed the limitations of socially situated artworks. Whilst *tenantspin* had been able to enhance relationships between tenants and local housing officers, it was, as demonstrated, ultimately powerless to influence broader trends in planning. At the moment that Dunn inherited the project from Superflex, he therefore also inherited a disenfranchised community and direct criticism from some tenants that the pilot project might have diverted attention from lobbying mechanisms that already existed, such as the High Rise Tenants Group which had formed by residents in 1991 to champion tenants rights. Many of the tenants across the different sites were ex-service men and women, or ex-union members adept at self-organisation, and if they had previously lacked the external audience that the internet provided, they were nevertheless already an 'empowered' community, capable of negotiating with housing authorities without the mediation of artists or facilitators.

Reactivating the project therefore also involved re-articulating what *tenantspin* could realistically achieve for its participants. Dunn, anticipating much future upheaval for tenants, believed that there was still a need for a project that could create a public forum for debate. The channel would be a means by which to raise important issues, but the project needed to be more realistic about its aims: accepting the patronage of HAT meant acknowledging that, despite Superflex's activist intentions, *tenantspin* was not being funded to initiate a full scale tenant-led revolt. Dunn understood that the project played an important social role, as a forum for interactions between the residents themselves, and that the studio could provide a context in which they could be playful as well as highlight the serious issues. The motives for resident involvement in the channel were diverse, and he needed to satisfy those who wanted to escape from the day-to-day concerns of the housing crisis as well as the lobbyists; he therefore initiated a formal split in programme content between social issues and artists' commissions. As he saw it, "There were grievances to air, life stories to share, songs to sing, spoons to play and a new approach to saying it all. What was needed, was someone quiet to make all the noise happen." Dunn thus worked with the legacy created by Superflex, testing out the real life, rather than symbolic, potential of a globally networked project.

Tenants continued to produce material on the very present issues raised by the housing debate, interviewing senior HAT officials, city council planners and local politicians but they were also encouraged to research and present programmes on other social issues of interest beyond their own immediate community. A key example was an interview between resident Brenda Tilsley and the vicar of a local church, which had become the focus of national media attention after the kidnap of Kenneth Bigley in Iraq, in 2004. In the course of the interview the vicar recounts how reactions to the kidnapping were misrepresented by the press, who even brought their own mourners to light candles and pose for photographs in order to portray the church as a local shrine. At moments like this, the potential in webcasting for presenting local perspectives more accurately, and resisting the stereotypes of mainstream media, becomes clear. Other key programmes from the period include webcasts on health, money and politics, all researched and delivered by the residents.

Exploring the channel as a new commissioning context for artists, Dunn invited local and international figures to respond to the project, with the central brief of collaborating with the residents. As well as tenant-led interviews with writer Will Self and anarchistic artist and creator of the KLF Bill Drummond, a live, multiple location performance work by Manchester-based artist Graham Parker was created which involved an A-Z, several taxis and the integral participation of an on-line audience. Dunn's aim was always to diverge as much as possible from the traditional model of reminiscence so often used with elderly communities, where the subjects presents their story but always defines themselves in relation to the past. Two key commissions that demonstrate this commitment include *tenantspin*'s participation in the EAST International 05 exhibition, Norwich Art Gallery, when the project was selected by artist Gustav Metzger, the originator of Auto-Destructive Art as an example of an artwork that operated as time and process-based in line with his own practice. Interviews were transmitted with Metzger, then in his eighties, alongside a debate on cryogenics with an enthusiast who had signed up for the procedure and who was interviewed by tenants Jean Niblock and John McGuirk. The second high profile commission was a collaboratively created BBC Radio 3 play, *SuperBlock*, developed with tenants by writer Jeff Young. This latter project imagined a distant future, which saw all of the demolished tower blocks, rebuilt one on top of the other like a postmodern Tower of Babel.

A ban on looking back meant that programming avoided the trap of nostalgia, encouraging the tenants to explore sometimes surreal ideas or comment on social issues as they occurred in the moment, rather than constantly repeat the same stories from their own past; this also created a space in which they could be something other than an elderly person defined by a community

Top Left
(Foreground) Sefton Park Community Centre and tower blocks. (2005).

55 — Standing in the way of control

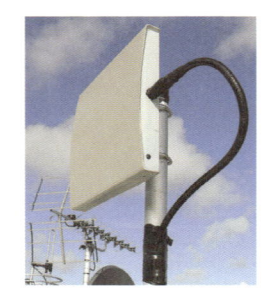

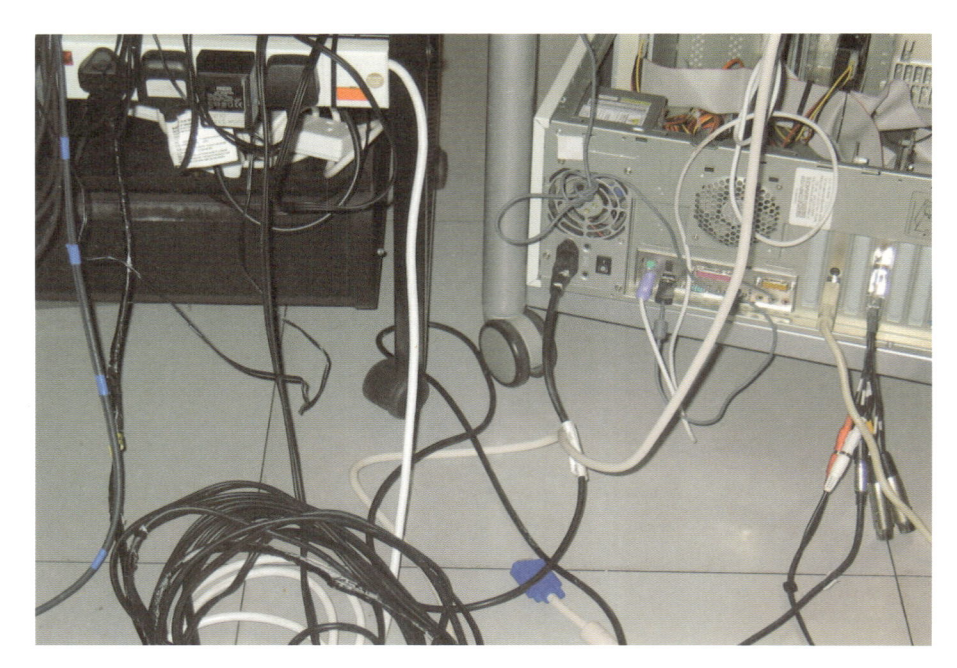

Top Left
Demolition film stills by Kath Healy (1999).

Top Middle
Short range AV transmitter, roof of Brompton House, Sefton Park (2005).

Far Right
tenantspin cables.

Right
Superflex: Rasmus Nielsen, Bjørnstjerne Christiansen and Jakob Fenger. Image courtesy of the artists.

housing crisis. Being in the moment also meant that the participants who took part over months and years had the opportunity to define that moment; Dunn felt there was an urgency for grass-roots projects to be active and visible in the run-up to the forthcoming Capital of Culture in 2008, a superstructure which imposed an idea of culture on the city, as much as it responded to what local artists and communities actually generated.

Artistic legacies

The project's social legacies, rather than changing the course of regeneration, can be identified as the public channel of communication that was opened up between tenants and their landlords; the interactions between the tenants and their wider global audience; and the relationships generated between the tenants themselves, many of whom met for the first time through *tenantspin* as the project broadened its reach across multiple sites. The artistic legacies of the project emerge out of a complex set of relationships between the tenants, Alan Dunn, the artists he invited to participate, and the process-based practice of Superflex, which frames the whole project.

At one level, Alan Dunn was, like the tenants and the project's patrons, one element within Superflex's 'social sculpture'. Yet, he was also far more than a locally based artist charged with facilitating community interactions whilst international artists travelled between other commitments. That particular role, so familiar to the commissioning structures of biennials, has its own implicit hierarchies with the local always subordinate to the international. Since Superflex had always intended to hand over the Liverpool branch of Superchannel, theirs was a planned absence and a deliberate letting go; it was in a large part down to Dunn's vision that *tenantspin* developed from faltering pilot to long-running project.

Whilst his creative input was integral to the project maintaining momentum, his was very much a behind-the-scenes practice, in contrast to the artists he invited to collaborate with the tenants who were visible through short projects that culminated publicly. He sought to engineer collaborations that were experimental contexts for artists to test out ideas but that were, at the same time, respectful of those who participated. He was wary of certain art world tendencies that fetishise amateur practices, re-framing hobbies as curiosities and non-art world professionals as naïve outsiders. It should also be noted that, through Superflex's patronage, *tenantspin* has been featured in several international museum shows and, to some extent, the project can never escape the fact that part of its appeal is the sight of 'ordinary' people performing within an art project. However, just as these contexts frame the participants, they in turn provide a framework for the artists and cultural specialists with whom they collaborate; never more so when the residents are hosting interviews, pursuing their own line of questioning with little regard for art-world status, in control of the situation which mediates them.

His was a role sometimes at odds with the institution that employed him; perhaps one of most contentious forms of institutional resistance instigated by Dunn was drawing back from multiple funders keen to attach themselves to the project. He successfully lobbied for Arena, the new housing association landlord that took over sites from LHAT, to take on the project as a core funder and to allow the project space to develop over time. He also turned down a bid from a major satellite channel that would have asked *tenantspin* to produce hours of rolling content; whilst visibility was important it was also equally important for the participants to have time away from the project and not to be constantly called upon to perform.

Alan Dunn's role within a bureaucratic system is reminiscent in many ways of the UK art collective and Beuys collaborators, the Artist Placement Group (APG). Formed in 1966, they situated artists inside corporations and government bodies in order to affect institutional systems. Always working with an open brief and an equivalent managerial salary, rather than a fee, artists were not compelled to make concrete art works but rather de-familiarise the normality of bureaucracy by their presence as a non-professional or 'incidental person'. According to one of the founders of APG, Barbara Steveni, the artist was charged with "repositioning art in the decision-making processes of society", with the context deciding half of the work. Whilst Dunn's brief was far from open, his position as an artist operating in an institutional context has parallels with the practices of the APG, through his challenging decision making processes and fighting for an autonomous space in which to make art which has repercussions in the world outside the gallery.

tenantspin is now managed by Arena Housing and FACT project managers Patrick Fox, Laura Yates and Ed Pink, and whilst no longer artist-led, the channel still commissions artists to collaborate on innovative projects for live transmission and the sharing of technological skills. A change in the demographic of participants has brought a renewed commitment to highlighting social issues. The project now involves tenants of all ages from across the 14,000 properties that Arena manage in the North West, a significant proportion of which have recently moved to the UK, in contrast to the original participants who were predominantly aged between fifty and ninety and were born and raised in Liverpool. New issues have arisen that are no longer focused around the urgency of social housing, but of citizenship. For example, in 2008, *tenantspin* participant Christian Ntirandekura, a Burundian national who had first sought asylum in the UK in 2004, was detained when he left a *tenantspin* workshop and eventually deported to Burundi, where he faced great danger both for past political actions and for the ethnic group to which he belongs. *tenantspin* provided an important lobbying group to bring his case to regional and national media attention, although ultimately this could no more stop his enforced repatriation than the pilot project could stop the demolition of the tower blocks. The sense in which the project now represents a wide community of interest without any other access to the mainstream media has however galvanised energies once more, and continued its relevance in an era where access to web presence is commonplace rather than exceptional.

In conclusion, whilst activist-style art practices such as Superflex's can no more affect social systems than agenda-laden institutional commissions, since neither have the power to alter economic conditions or deep-seated social inequalities, the *tenantspin* project ultimately had, and still has, more than a symbolic value. The project provides a platform for residents to ask challenging questions of contemporary social and cultural agendas, produce their own visions of the future and raise issues of pressing concern that might otherwise fall out of the range of the authorities' radar.

tenantspin is ultimately as much an example of community activism as it is an example of 21st Century 'social sculpture'. Whilst DIY aesthetics come in and out of fashion in the art world, the communities of interest grouped around the project will continue to participate as long as there is still a purpose in their being seen and heard in this century.

w. *www.tenantspin.org*

Marie-Anne McQuay is a freelance curator and writer based in London and Liverpool.

Singing the sound of silence

Alan Dunn

> In a talk at ZKM Gallery in Karlsruhe in March 2001, David Harding recounts the tale of Douglas Gordon being asked by a curator, "What were you taught in the Environmental Art Department?", and Douglas replying, "To sing. Not how to sing but simply, to sing." I understand this, but I think that I learnt something different in my time in Environmental Art — the same time as Douglas — and that was to keep quiet.

It seemed important to me to step back from situations and quietly observe, whether that be in and around the murals in South Chicago, on scaffolding attached to the gable-ends of Blackhill, Glasgow amongst the complex words and ideas of Richard De Marco or John Latham, visiting the Barlinnie Special Unit in Wormwood Scrubbs, walking through East Berlin before re-unification or making the long trips to experience the National Review of Live Art in London.

We were asked to find our own relationships with different social situations, and I took this to understand that as 'social artists' we needn't always be in the centre of it all.

I left Environmental Art in 1991 and spent ten years away from Glasgow, 'in the field', working on an enormous mural in Hamilton, public interventions on the Raffles Estate in Carlisle, billboard posters with the Great North Run in Newcastle, posters with the Big Issue In The North, in Manchester, projects with schools in Cologne, Salford and Washington DC, hoardings and banners as part of Euro '96, artworks with Wirral Drug Services, The Domino and Bowling Club of Widnes, The European Special Olympics, education work for the Tate Gallery, co-curating The Liverpool Billboard Project and some University work.

When handed the keys to the *tenantspin* project in May 2001, the vehicle had just been assembled, revved up once and then left, uncertain who could drive it or even which direction it could point. It had been set up by FACT, Superflex and HAT as an idealistic model for social change, bringing together elderly people with streaming technology, a real housing development programme and an enthusiastic arts agency.

There were grievances to air, life stories to share, songs to sing, spoons to play and a new approach to saying it all. What was needed, was someone quiet to make all this noise happen. In my *tenantspin* interview, when asked to describe some recent works that informed my thinking, I mentioned a little known piece by Douglas comprising the words, 'A minute's silence', that appeared silently on an outdoor screen for sixty seconds, still my favourite work of his.

I was to be Malcolm McLaren bringing his New York Dolls ideas to London, with hopes of changing the system, and Sir Alex Ferguson arriving in Manchester to build on his work at Aberdeen. Whereas my Grandfather worked in the Govan shipyard near Ferguson's house, he was, unlike Ferguson, a totally silent man all his life, getting on with the job and trying to get along with people. Yet he helped create some extraordinary structures in which other people journeyed.

FACT's founder, Eddie Berg, called me into his office on my first day and outlined a desire for *tenantspin* to become an internationally-known model for good practice in the field of technology, social engagement, sustainable work, high quality commissioning and media art.

Such ambition for a 'community project', and this before access to broadband, Liverpool's European Capital of Culture status or even the FACT Centre. I shared Eddie's belief that the ingredients were there for something radical.

And *tenantspin* did become everything Eddie dreamt of. We took risks, had fun, inspired thousands, changed hundreds of lives, had bundles of PhDs written about us, surprised ourselves, made some noise, confused some people and left some silence. I recently heard that the filmmaker David Lynch has been watching *tenantspin* webcasts from his base in Hollywood. I also worked in a remote part of Cumbria recently, and the people there had heard of *tenantspin*. I took enquiries from the outback of Australia from someone "wanting a *tenantspin*", and we presented work in India, Brazil, Korea, across Europe, America and the South Pole.

A *tenantspin* participant bizarrely even made it on to the Eurovision Song Contest, representing Britain in Latvia, in 2003. Unfortunately, that was the year there were claims that the sound had been sabotaged.

Still, even out-of-synch singing doesn't get in the way of a good *tenantspin* story.

Left
Sunday Matinee The Red Day launch, Foreign Investment [detail]. (2003).

Top
Will Self and Josie Crawford interview. (2002).

nomadic practices often result in immaterial or transient work rather than fixed and tangible objects. Rather than thinking about working creatively within a given environment or space — the studio or gallery — it is more important to identify places and environments that can be creatively explored, spaces that themselves form the starting point and the raw material for the creative work done in them. ' Extending from place to place, the work is an open-ended activity, conducted across media and locations. Place is mobilized: the site is no longer a singular location but a way-station in a circuit of passage.'[5]

Joseph Beuys, noted for his extension of art into performance, politics and anthropology, famously advocated that everyone is an artist. The philosopher Paul Virilio's echo of this is that everywhere is art — or that art is everywhere, all the time: 'The art of today with its interactive techniques has now reached the level of instantaneous exchange between actor and spectator, the final delocalisation. The presence of art, and therefore its localisation, is threatened. And yet that's exactly where the solution to the threat lies, in the question of the temporality of art today. We have attained the limit of velocity, the capacity for ubiquity, for instantaneousness and immediacy.'[6]

This connects with aspects of the curator Nicolas Bourriaud's sense of 'relational æsthetics' (manifest in his book of that name and in his curatorial strategies) wherein he suggests that, 'in the era of simultaneous communication, forms only take shape in online time; they can be re-activated at will and are subject to change. The object is no longer materially or conceptually defined but relationally. What is produced are connections with the world broadcast by the object.'[7] So, having been, in Virilio's term, delocalised, the spatial location of art has increasingly been replaced by an emphasis on its location in time, emphasising art as trajectory rather than destination, and on the act not its product. As Daniel Buren put it, 'the desertion of the studio allows every day, every place, every human interaction to become a fundamental part of the work'.[8] This sentiment is echoed in the influential American artist and educator John Baldessari's claim that art education might as well take place 'sitting on a log' as in a studio or anywhere else because, 'it's a people-oriented activity'.[9]

And now, of course, sitting on a log with a laptop and a mobile phone, would enable a potentially limitless reach for the interaction. It is possible to conceive of the SuperCity art school as a series of sites equivalent to Baldessari's log, acting as hubs of communication between each other and the rest of the world, providing spaces for thinking, making and talking that could be simultaneously intimate and expansive. For the current art schools, particularly those in the 'new university' sector, to function in this way, though, would require a radical de-centralisation and freeing of their bureaucratic structure that is hard to envisage.

Baldessari's seemingly throwaway remark is important in suggesting that, in the context of art education, people are more important than the places they occupy. And so, in the persistent climate of shrinking resources for art schools in which compromises have to be made, more people in less space is a better option than more space with less people. The space of the art school in this model is the space of dialogue, a place for people to generate, share and debate ideas. The things that provoke those ideas and the things that might be made in response to them are fundamental, but the site of their creation and manufacture is as likely to be outside the walls of the art school as within, and arguably will be of more social value as 'art' if it is. 'I'm less interested in what art is than in what isn't art yet. What really interests me is how you move stuff into the area of art that isn't there,' says Baldessari.

Such a space for dialogue, an open, generous and sociable space, suggests that a model for contemporary art practice and education should be located in contemporary society itself, particularly in how and what we communicate, and in what happens to us in the process of that communication. Such an approach would emphasise the relationship between the production, transmission and reception of art, emphasising the artist's role as a communicator, collaborator and facilitator as much as a maker. Bourriaud's notion of the relational advocates an art that takes as its theoretical and practical point of departure the social context of human relationships rather than the specific, individual or private space. He defines relational æsthetics as consisting in the judgement of artworks on the basis of the inter-human relations they represent, produce or prompt. Art on this basis emphasises the human activity or performativity of making, a view of art as a process, a way of being and acting crucially rooted in the world around us, in which the physical and the social world are simultaneously the subject, the material and the object of the work.

This is a fundamentally social model of creativity, and as such positions itself contrary to the romantic notion of the lone artist as the archetype of heroic individualism, and art as the means of individual emotional expression, an image that persists not only in general public perception and the popular media, but also still in too many aspects of institutionalised art education. But such an outward-looking approach to art does not deny the introspection that is often held to be at its heart. In the words of one of TS Elliot's poems, 'We shall not cease from exploration, and the end of our exploring will be to arrive where we started and know the place for the first time'.[10] In this spirit of creativity as invest-igation, art education should be rooted in collaborative engagement and selfdiscovery, whether in the production of works of collective author-

ship, or in personal and individual work that never loses sight of its complex relationship to a wider world. This involves recognising that interaction, communication and collective experience are fundamental to making cultural activity meaningful, and in turn invites a participatory form of spectatorship, aspiring to generate in its audience an engagement and interaction with the work that goes beyond passive consumption.

And so, a manifesto for the SuperCity art school might advocate:

— Education as a web of relationships between investigation, production, transmission and reception, spread across a geographical network that would turn the existing university departments and art schools into satellites throughout the SuperCity and beyond.

— Promoting communication, collaboration, curating, and facilitation as much as making.

— Encouraging insistently individual forms of expression but within the fold of a collective endeavour.

— Making and presenting work in ways and in places that encourage discussion, promote dialogue and enable exchange, collaboration and mutual support.

— Identifying a plethora of environments that can be creatively explored rather than requiring students to explore creatively within a fixed environment.

— Using space in ways that question possession and individual occupation, promoting strategies in which space is used in progressive ways, constantly transforming it, occupying and re-occupying, filling and emptying, emphasising 're-use' rather than 'use'.

— Promoting local, national and international dialogue and collaboration with other students and artists, and with other individuals and organisations within and beyond the 'artworld'.

Recalling the philosopher Bertrand Russell's In Praise of Idleness,[11] such an art school would embrace a purposeful purposelessness and assert that art and its teaching should be based on exploration more than definition, pragmatism rather than dogma, and questioning rather than assertion. It would work on an understanding that collaboration should take precedence over self-expression, that anything's use is more important than its ownership, action is more important than rhetoric, the transient is as significant as the permanent, and that improvisation is as important as intention. There is a fundamental educational and creative value in not always knowing what one is doing, and the SuperCity art school would provide the space, actual and metaphorical, in which to do it.

Derek Horton is an artist, writer and teacher. Formerly head of research in contemporary art at Leeds Metropolitan University, he co-founded the online magazines /seconds with Peter Lewis in 2005 and Soanyway with Lisa Stansbie in 2009.

[1] Kaprow coined the term 'Happenings' and, along with Watts and Brecht, was one of the founders of the Fluxus group of artists who took a playful approach to everyday materials and situations. In the geographical context of SuperCity it is interesting to note that Brecht, Robert Filliou and a number of other prominent Fluxus artists were regular visiting tutors at Leeds Polytechnic in the late 60's and early 70's when the Fluxus artist Robin Page taught in Leeds.

[2] Peter Boswell, 'Bruce Conner, Theater of Light and Shadow', in 2000 BC: The Bruce Conner Story Part II, Minneapolis: Walker Art Center, 2000.

[3] Daniel Buren, 'The Function of the Studio', Frieze, October, Vol 10, Fall 1979 (pp 51-58).

[4] Daniel Buren, op cit.

[5] Robert Smithson, 'Site, Non-site', in Robert Smithson: The Collected Writings, Berkeley: University of California Press, 1996.

[6] Paul Virilio, in 'The Dark Spot of Art', a conversation between Catherine David and Paul Virilio [trans. Brian Holmes], Documenta X, Documents 1, Kassel: Cantz Verlag, 1997.

[7] Nicolas Bourriaud, Relational æsthetics, [trans. Simon Pleasance & Fronza Woods], Dijon: Les Presses du Reel, 2002.

[8] Daniel Buren, in his lecture 'The Desertion of the Studio and its Implications', at the University of Southern California School of the Arts, Los Angeles, 8 April 2003, transcribed from my own notes of the event.

[9] See John Baldessari's contribution to the Tate symposium Rethinking Arts Education for the Twenty-First Century, 16 July 2005, partially documented as a podcast at: www.tate.org.uk/onlineevents/webcasts/rethinking_arts_education/default.jsp

[10] TS Elliot, Four Quartets, No 4, 'Little Gidding', (1942) reprinted in TS Elliot, Complete Poems and Plays, London: Faber & Faber, 2004.

[11] Bertrand Russell, In Praise of Idleness, (1935), London: Routledge, 1994.

(Sitting on a log)
Imagining the SuperCity Art School

Derek Horton

In the economic downturn of 2008/2009 only farming and education sustained percentage growth in the UK economy, due in no small part to key-workers exiting failing business, arts and science sectors and seeking sanctuary in the relative security of the education system. What better time for a re-appraisal of the current state of that system and a fresh look at what can be done to shake up and wake up this potential powerhouse (and birthplace) of the creative economy of the SuperCity? In a thought-provoking article that casts a contemporary eye on the past whilst seeking out new adventures in modern thinking, Derek Horton provides an outline for a radicalised education model that could just see us through into the 22nd Century.

The architect Will Alsop's vision of a Northern super-city is one that invites speculation about how people might want to live their lives in the future. He envisages the apparently inconceivable precisely in order to allow us to conceive the possibility of a different way of urban and suburban life. The material transformation of the infrastructure that it proposes inevitably suggests a new vision for the civic and cultural infrastructure too.

What if the SuperCity were to have an art school. Imagining the art schools of Liverpool, Manchester, Leeds and Hull and the cities of Ireland, Holland and Denmark (as well as those of the smaller towns along the Corridor) as satellites of the SuperCity's art school requires an equivalent suspension of disbelief, even more so given that most are currently no longer 'art schools' as such but subsumed in the unwieldy mega-bureaucracies of the so-called 'new' universities. In the current climate, where education is commodified in response to a society that is acquisitive but not inquisitive, competition for students and status always trumps intellectual collaboration, rhetorical PR conceals pedagogical inadequacy, funding streams determine research and every kind of resource is subject to ever more stringent financial constraint; so what better time to suspend disbelief for long enough to imagine an alternative future for art education in the 21st Century? Fundamental to such an imaginative leap might be a recognition that the interaction between individuals and organisations that occurs through making art happen can bring about real transformation in those individuals and organisations and, as a consequence, in the wider culture of which they are part.

In 1957, Allan Kaprow, Robert Watts and George Brecht [1] proposed an experimental laboratory for producing art relating to the everyday, in contrast to the 'sublime' that preoccupied their contemporaries in the New York School. The loosening of forms, randomness, boundlessness and casual improvisation they proposed are characteristic of much art and art education that took place during the 1960's and 70's. In British art education, some of the perceived negative aspects of these developments, together with changes in the political and educational climate of the 1980's and 90's, saw the decline of such approaches in a 'return to order', but many have now concluded that a sturdy baby was thrown out with this bath water. For all its shortcomings, in its utopian ambition, its disregard for disciplinary boundaries and its faith in the human capacity for creativity and the liberating potential of its mobilisation, the 60's and 70's experiment represented a dynamic model for cultural engagement. The focus of the SuperCity art school might well be, therefore, on a re-assessment of its ideas and values.

'The assumptions and conventions of the art world are as much a material for art as pencil, pen, paint or found objects.' [2]

This statement, made about the American artist and filmmaker Bruce Conner, might usefully be applied more generally to thinking about the function and indeed the curriculum of a purposeful art school. Bringing taken-for-granted assumptions into sharp focus and questioning their validity is central to cultural activity and is surely one of the most important functions of art education. The conventional practice of controlling, defining and occupying spaces for both the making and showing of art, privileges the idea of the artwork as a tangible object, created in the space of the studio and exhibited in the space of the gallery. This often serves to marginalise the activity-centred, process-based or socially-engaged propositions that characterise much contemporary practice, in which making 'things' is just one option amongst many available to artists, and in which the gallery exhibition is only one of a diversity of platforms of visibility for their work.

Questioning art's need for the production of material objects and the unique value it places on them involves, of course, a concomitant questioning of the role of physical space, not least in challenging the idea that studio space and gallery space are the primary sites of production and visibility for art.

'The seemingly innocuous term, "studio", remains stubbornly in place despite the interrogations of successive modernist avant-gardes, the pressures of technological change and the influences of post-modern theory... A cursory examination reveals a complex legacy of received beliefs and images dating back to the Renaissance. What does this continued and prevalent use mean? An instance of desirable, perhaps even necessary, continuity in the face of adversity? Or a failure of the imagination, a failure to grasp the implications and potential of changing conditions in which contemporary art and design is, or could be, made or produced?' [3]

The French artist Daniel Buren asked this question in 1979, in his article 'The Function of the Studio', and his two opposing answers to his own question characterise a fundamental debate in art education that persists thirty years later. Despite, or maybe even because of, the increasingly market-driven financial management of higher education that continually demands 'efficiency-savings' in space, many art educators still fight for the preservation of traditional studio space, with an in-built assumption that the bigger it is the better it is, as a necessary continuity in the face of adversity. Surely now, more than a generation later, a forward-looking art school must take up Buren's challenge and have the imagination to grasp the implications and potential of the changed conditions in which art is now made?

Buren proposed that it was what he called 'the art of yesterday' for which the studio was 'an essential, even unique, place of production', and that all his work 'proceeded from its extinction'. [4] Whilst operating without a conventional studio, Buren's primarily object-based material practice now itself appears like the art of yesterday — or at least rather less than radical — in a world where, although the studio is still far from extinct, artists increasingly use social spaces, virtual space, personal space and global space in ways that have no dependency on, nor even necessarily any connection with, the traditional studio or gallery. Such

The House on the Borderland: Lesley Young, James Hutchinson and the Salford Restoration Office

Laura Mansfield

The Salford Restoration Office sits at 142 Chapel Street on the boundary between Manchester and Salford. It is an unassuming, compact space that is reminiscent of so many part-converted, part-abandoned transitional shop spaces that festoon the urban landscape of cities across the region. It has been an artist's studio, an art gallery and, of course, a shop. It is rented from an architect, who lives next door. This set of conditions in many ways mirrors what the Salford Restoration Society does itself. Laura Mansfield takes a critical look.

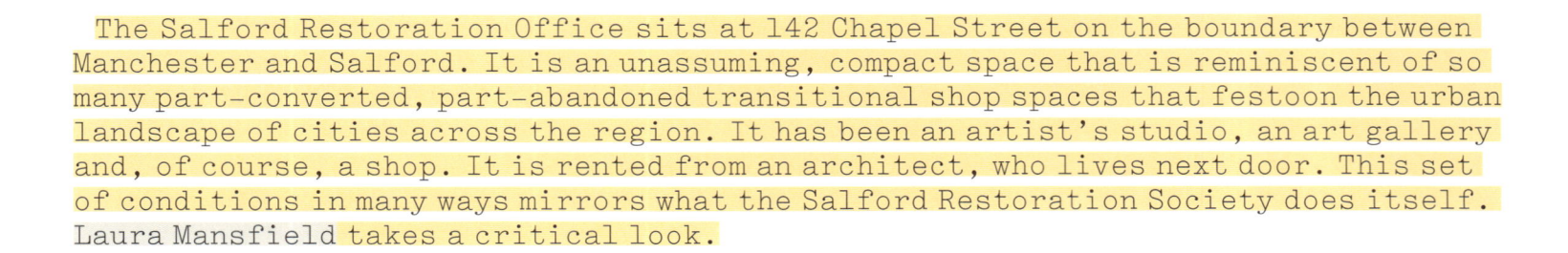

Lesley Young and James Hutchinson are hotwired into the ecology of the cities of Salford and Manchester. As founders and prime movers behind the nebulous Salford Restoration Office, they are on a mission to join up the dots between the artistic community and the placement, ambition and accessibility of cultural institutions in the city and beyond. Formed in February 2007, the Office wants to see the production of good art. Where, how, with whom and in what context this art gets made drives the Office into territories not traditionally understood as the remit of artists, and more akin to the remit of policy makers, arts councils and local government. By claiming these territories as a legitimate material for their creativity they radicalise acts more usually seen as bureaucratic, obstructive and dull and turn them into viable, invigorated tools for the creation, critique and discussion of art.

"We established a set of parameters that we wanted to work within. We were interested in focusing on Manchester and Salford and the institutions within them, thinking about these places as sites for production alongside an awareness that there is an artistic community in the cities which is effected by the institutions, either for good or for bad. We were interested in that interrelationship."

The Office takes as its starting point the premise that the interrelationship of cultural institutions in the cities are in need of being broken open, and that in doing so it is possible to release the energy held within it.

"We began by thinking about the infrastructure as being a functioning machine".

In breaking open the machine they create a new energy within the different cultural mechanisms of the cities, opening up the existing structures to create new networks and paths of interaction, areas ripe for artistic engagement and sites where new and exciting propositions can come to fruition.

The Office's modus operandi is to offer its services to institutions as an agency that investigates problems identified within an organisation. In its first two years it worked with Manchester Metropolitan University, Manchester University, Castlefield Gallery, The Whitworth Art Gallery, and Cornerhouse to initiate projects that investigate, critique and engage with an identifiable (and often invisible) problem area. The resolution can take a variety of forms. It can be a group discussion, an exhibition, a new administrative framework for an organisation, or a vigorous shake-up of an existing framework.

This attempt to re-engage the artistic with the institution on a discursive level is a process that echoes the influential work of the The Art Workers' Coalition. Formed in 1969, in New York, the coalition was an open collective of artists, filmmakers, writers, critics, and museum staff whose principle aim was to pressure the city's museums into implementing reforms and reinvigorating their seemingly turgid exhibitions policy. Initiated when the artist George Takis removed one of his sculptures from display in the Museum of Modern Art following a disagreement on the conditions of its exhibition, the coalition drew attention to the conditions cultural practitioners found themselves operating within and the dominant control of the museum over the reception and display of their work. A further parallel could be drawn between the Office and the British Artists Placement Group. The APG placed artists within bureaucratic institutions from government departments to engineering plants, giving the artists a role as both an advisor and observer, using the creativity of art in contexts outside the traditional barriers of the cultural institution. In a contemporary take, the Office is using such a precedent within the framework of the cultural institution itself; the arts institution having become increasingly professionalised and bureaucratised in line with government policy and funding criteria.

In an ongoing project with the Whitworth Art Gallery, the Office formed the 'Whitworth Cabinet'; a structure where a collection of twelve individuals from across the cultural spectrum — artists, curators, writers, and theorists — would regularly meet and steer the development of the administrative framework, by introducing new practices, suggesting alternatives and advising on the existing structures. The members of the Cabinet would rotate, keeping the structure vibrant and enabling a continual flow of new ideas and responses.

"The Whitworth Cabinet was set up to explore the institution and challenge its working method. It is not visible to an audience, its existence is an attempt to affect the balance of the institution from within"

In their most recent project, for the launch of the Research Institute for Cosmopolitan Cultures, opening at the University of Manchester, the Office invited Danish artist Katya Sander to develop a new work. Sander produced five thousand pin-badges bearing the phrase 'If you read this, I'll give it to you (but then you must wear it)'. Each badge represents a social contract between those who wear it, and those who act upon its statement in order to acquire it, marking a chain of interrelationships throughout the cities of Manchester and Salford. To mark the opening of the new research centre, individuals working in higher education organisations and art spaces across Manchester distributed the badges freely. By starting with an individual embedded in the institutional structure of the cities, the badges subsequently filtered out into new networks of city users, conceptually opening up the institutional frameworks to new possibilities of dialogue, discussion and potential users.

Sander says: "The distribution of the badges is orchestrated to bring about a discussion about the 'knowledge economy' and 'education industry' that many post-industrial cities have invested in... I believe that knowledge and education remain empowering. This project attempts to link educational institutions (and the many bodies that pass through them every day) to a discussion about public space, a relationship particularly pertinent in the context of 'cosmopolitan culture'."

At a Symposium held at the Witte de With institute of artistic research in Rotterdam, Young and Hutchinson were invited to discuss notions of 'embedded' curation — a practice of curation where the individual curator immerses him or herself in a specific territory, or local context, and works extensively within this framework, rather than the more traditional model that sees artists moving between cities, countries and sites looking for new opportunities to display a body of work. Young and Hutchinson's formation of the Salford Restoration Office reflects an embedded ethos, working specifically within the boundaries of Greater Manchester and the local arts networks, finding intriguing and exciting opportunities for arts production.

One such project was Centrifuge, an experimental artists' development scheme formed on behalf of Manchester Metropolitan University and the university consortium, Northern Edge. The Office was asked to find a way to help art school graduates who had chosen to base themselves in the North to develop skills that would allow them to operate confidently and critically in the

Far Left
Salford Restoration Office, front of building.
Stephen Iles

Left
Lesley Young and James Hutchinson at 'The Curators', Rotterdam Dialogues: Critics, Curators, Artists, Witte de With, Rotterdam, March 2009. Image: Barnaby Drabble.

Right
Centrifuge meeting at Documenta 12, Kassel, August 2007.

region, and to encourage them to find space for themselves and their ideas in a challenging and unpredictable professional climate. Working collaboratively with the Office the group of participating young artists considered what they wanted to explore, and then came up with a structure through which to do it. They took the notion of an Art Prize as their starting point. The model of an Art Prize enabled the group to examine the power structures and bureaucracies they found themselves operating within as artists and organisers, thinking about and responding to possibilities for an alternative form of prize.

In being faced with the layers of institutional networks surrounding their individual practices, as well as their desire for recognition as artists, Centrifuge generated an environment that encouraged the participating artists to find a voice that was not solely theirs to control, and encouraged the artists to accumulate knowledge of their individual situations and generate discussion with regards to their future. The Office invited artists Imogen Stidworthy and Dirk Fleischmann to act as moderators to these discussions, assisting the group's investigations.

The Art Prize structure was a means to critique the current forms of artistic development put in place, and develop alternative structures and networks for artistic production. The Prize did not generate any winners or even a competition, but functioned solely as a structure within which discussion could take place. As Young and Hutchinson note, the Art Prize project functioned as a means to "remind the participants that although the (art) world they live in appears to be set up as a competition, the conventions are theirs to use and to change as they please." It is through the process of discussion and critique that valuable dialogues are formed, which in turn, have the potential to liberate both artists and institutions from conventional modes of engagement and production.

With each new project or commission, Young and Hutchinson develop their ideas and processes of engagement. Their end result is never pre-planned or pre-empted, it is only through its process that the project evolves into its eventual outcome, creating new threads of discussion and interpretation. Through their discursive and open working method the Office effectively cultivates a healthy economy of ideas in the cultural networks of Manchester and Salford, offering up possibilities of change and development.

Laura Mansfield is a critical writer and curator who has contributed to AN Magazine, Circa and Arty Magazine and delivered papers on the work of artist Daphne Wright.

61 — The House on the Borderland

Advertisement

Castlefield Gallery

exhibitions △ events △ performances △ talks
screenings △ artists' professional development
www.castlefieldgallery.co.uk △ www.theartguide.co.uk

2 Hewitt Street Manchester M15 4GB UK

Supported by ARTS COUNCIL ENGLAND

photo: jamie crawford

---

soanyway

Soanyway is a magazine of words, pictures and sound that tell stories.

Regularly updated at
www.soanyway.org.uk

"There's a thousand sides to everything – not just heroes and villains. So anyway, … so anyway, … so anyway…"So anyway" ought to be one word. Like a place or a river… Soanyway River."

Zabriskie Point, 1970, Michelangelo Antonioni

Published and edited by Derek Horton and Lisa Stansbie

dust

dust — a commercial arts & design practice 'fuelled by non-commercial activity, defined by the FLUX of intuition, TEXTURE of process and the MEANS to produce on a whim'.

Book & Publication Design

www.studio-dust.com   i@studio-dust.com
tweet:@dustcollective

estd. TURN OF THE CENTURY, SHEFFIELD UK

CERI HAND GALLERY

Representing the following artists:

**DOUG JONES
ELEANOR MORETON
HENNY ACLOQUE
JEN LIU
MATTHEW HOULDING
MEL BRIMFIELD
MIMEI THOMPSON
NICK CROWE & IAN RAWLINSON
REBECCA LENNON
S MARK GUBB
SAMANTHA DONNELLY**

Ceri Hand Gallery
+44 (0)151 207 0899
info@cerihand.co.uk
www.cerihand.co.uk

Jackson Pollock the Musical
A book by Roger McKinley

Winner of the Urbis 'Best of Manchester Awards 2007 — Visual Arts Category'.

Jackson Pollock the Musical is a tragic-comic, imaginary musical journey to discover the nature of the greatest American painter of the 20th Century, his death by car crash and his continuation in the Underworld.

With eighteen original songs, Jackson Pollock the Musical is a libretto for a musical based on the life and times of this Abstract Expressionist painter.

"I have always found Jackson Pollock the most interesting Abstract Expressionist and a drunken and tragic figure. I hope this book has a deserved success." George Melly

£9.99
ISBN 978-0-9552672-1-5

Available from bookshops or directly from www.jacksonpollockthemusical.com

mb

Michael Butterworth
michaelbutterworthbooks@googlemail.com

Advertisement

The place to buy art in Manchester and the North.

24—27 September 2009
Urbis, Manchester

Visit **www.buyartfair.co.uk** to pre-register for your free tickets (£5/£4 on the door).

Sponsored by **Bluefin** and **AXA ART**

STOREY GALLERY

A contemporary art organisation based in Lancaster, which commissions, promotes and presents a programme by nationally and internationally significant artists.

www.storeygallery.org.uk

Advertisement

FERAL TRADE
IMPORT-EXPORT
Since 2003

www.feraltrade.org   kate@feraltrade.org

FERAL TRADE
SUMMER '09 PRODUCT LINE

Imported from source and distributed UK, Europe & Americas using the surplus freight potential of commuter, vacation, social and curatorial traffic for strategic movement of goods. Products in current circulation: coffee from El Salvador, tea from Bangladesh, salt from Gujarat, couscous from Morocco, hot chocolate from Oaxaca and turkish delight from Montenegro.

Track all shipments at **www.feraltrade.org/tracking**